THE 20TH CENTURY

. . .

THE REAL TRUTH

ROBERT HUBSCHMAN

iUniverse books may be ordered through booksellers or by contacting:

iUniverse
1663 Liberty Drive
Bloomington, IN 47403
www.iuniverse.com
1-800-Authors (1-800-288-4677)

ISBN: 978-1-5320-3071-0 (sc)
ISBN: 978-1-5320-3072-7 (e)

Print information available on the last page.

iUniverse rev. date: 08/21/2017

Contents

Executive Consultants:

Sanford Hubschman

Ward Davis

Michele Davis

Preface

There has never been a time that has mirrored the recorded advancements and the growth of humanity in the ten decades known has the 20th century. Nowhere in known recorded history of humanity can even come close to human development in nearly every single industry could come close to the changes accomplished in a worldwide scenario like that in comparison to the 20th century. As an avid reader, I have always enjoyed a great book and authors. I know that my interests have varied to almost every field imaginable from non-fiction to science fiction; just as the Holy Bible to Star Wars and almost everything in between. As I got older and in all reality, did everything late in life in comparison to people of my age group; the best example is earning my Master's Degree in my late 40's. I noticed that my hunger for knowledge did increase with age and I do find myself a student in all history; especially the history of humanity.

There are several people who are my inspiration for such an undergoing of writing the real truths about the 20th century and foremost must be my parents, who really lived the life for most of the century. They always inspired me to shoot for the stars and are the smartest people that I have ever known. The second must be the support of the rest of my family; especially my sister (Michele) and her husband (Ward). They pushed me to first write this dream and fed me with ideas and technological development. I wish to thank my other sister (Ann Marie), my two nephews (Joel and Kevin), my niece, her husband and my brother's granddaughter (Anya, Enrique and Kalayna) for their ideas and support. The main source for this undertaken was inspired by my Primary Care Physician, DR. Todd K. Rosenthal; who gave me the idea when he brought in his laptop, instead of a chart for a normal examination. A special thank you to my Aunt Pat, Uncle Angie, Aunt Sally (RIP), Uncle Allen and one of my family's best friend; Mr. Jabs; for all their input and inspiration; plus, my Beloved Aunt Theresa, wished I listened to you 30 years ago. The fact that this list can grow with the rest of my family and friends; but my real true Inspiration (The Blessed Mother). It seems like She has been influencing me in every way imaginable, almost to the point that some of my ideas are really beyond my thoughts. I take the philosophy of who I consider the greatest brain of the 20ᵗʰ century, Albert Einstein, who only lived 55 years into the century, about Religion and Science. His quote about Religion and Science is so true, insomuch "Science without Religion is lame and Religion without Science is blind." All I can say is Thank You, Blessed Mother Mary for all Your help. I know that I am not worthy, but I hope that this pleases You, Jesus and God.

The Blessed Mother's appearance a hundred years ago to three small children in Fatima, where She predicted both World Wars is well documented by believers and so-called non-believers. War World I took place within the year of Her appearance and World War II took place nearly 22 years later. She warned that God was not happy with the world and the direction it was heading. One must wonder is He any happier with us in the last hundred years? As illustrated above and throughout, one can marvel at our advancements but at what cost? We really did not have peace since Her Appearance and as a world on a whole, we are denying His Existence and drifting further away from Him. There are over 2 billion Catholics and Christians in the world combined; and almost every other Faiths and cultures that recorded His Son's (or Great Prophet) Existence.

The final tribute must go to God and His Only Son Jesus Christ. He really must be truly A Loving and Caring God to put up with us, His creation for so long. His Love must be endless and forever everlasting, insomuch to look down and see what a mess we made of all the gifts that He has given us. We are so pompous and arrogant to think that science can make the body parts, but those of us that still have love for Him and commonsense ask; What about the souls? I like to dedicate this to my brother (Alan). Rest in Peace Little brother!! You should be proud especially of your daughter, her husband and your precious beautiful granddaughter; she looks just like you!!

Chapter 1

The History and Overview

This publication is intended to be an educational learning tool to highlight how our society has advanced due to the many influences produced in the 20th century. It seems that each industry has had a hand in each other industry's advancements, which seems to have no boundaries in the growth potential. The next couple of chapters will be a review of the culture and philosophy. These subjects are so close in the realm of relationship to each other and some subject matter may seem redundant, but in some experts' view philosophy is often the population's reaction to events that take place in a culture and the reasoning for such occurrences. This can often be associated with ideology, which can be how a population reacts within their individual culture and how each culture relates to other cultures. Although there will be some opinions expressed in some subjects within the scope of being morally and ethically right, but in all reality, there will be a concentrated effort to convey the whole truth.

It seems that anytime that there is an effort to write anything historical, there is always an attempt to put opinion and normally only half the facts are relatively revealed. With some exceptions, there will be a concentrated effort to convey the whole story or facts concerning the 20th century and the influences felt in the first part of the 21st century. It seems that every author is somewhat influenced by his or her life experiences and the human factor or scenario finds its way into the publication. This is really no exception and to point this fact out at the onset is being honest. The changes through technology and advancement, which engulfed our society locally, nationally and even globally was a complete phenomenon in the 20th century. As mentioned in the preface, the changes in the medical field alone speaks volumes of these advancements. Who would have thought that one can get virtually every organ transplanted within the last few decades? The changes between 1900 to 2000AD are both astronomically and unbelievable. To point at one individual for these advancements would be unreasonable and unfair. The list of individuals in all fields and acknowledge or give them just credit would probably or properly documented fill several books. As each of these brilliant minds shared his or her own contribution(s), which undoubtedly shaped our lives in the 20th century and beyond. The slogan, which will be used so many times, in both illustrates to follow and beyond documenting the 20th century and our future is really an understatement and that is 'Necessity is the Mother of Invention.' This theme will be repeated several times because it is so truthful and it best describes the era in question.

As stated the list of minds are almost endless and one can almost write a novel size book rivaling War and Peace, highlighting their genius and change because of just their insight, ability to dream and what they projected for the future. To list or highlight just certain individuals would be just the revealing the tip of the iceberg of individuals, who had the brilliance in every industry imaginable both realized and will soon established on a global scale. The list of some individuals will be noted in upcoming chapters, but the list will be incomplete because of the several numbers as stated above. It is important to note that changes were going to take place in nearly every established industry at the turn of the century and new industries were on the horizon as we progressed through the century. Through this progression, it would be mindful that some industries became obsolete, matured to another level or replaced by a new concept due to technological advancements and/or consumer demand. The adage stated above about necessity never held truer than the inventions, technology and advancements that shaped the 20th century.

The most significant change that must be hard to imagine is the world to an average child, whereas they have not really witnessed the advancements in comparison to their parents, grandparents and even their great grandparents. For them to grasp the concept that at the start of the 20th century that the world was limited to perhaps their or a neighbor's farm, unless their family was fortunate to live by a town and in some rare scenarios by a city in certain parts of the country; especially the United States. The lifestyle was still very much in the agricultural stages and as illustrated cities were widespread, with some industrial industries just in their infancy; while others would be documented in the science fiction category. Even the professional sporting world of Major League Baseball and the National Football League first established and existed in areas with geographical limitations. Initially, the mid part of the United States would be as far as they would extend because of transportation issues. As illustrated above farming and agriculture were the business norms for most of the United States, along with mining and the occasional gold rushes in primarily California and Alaska at the start of the century.

As for the European Continent, most countries operated very differently than the concept in the United States, whereas most businesses were specialized. The days and hours of operation or being open to the public also differed in many respects. Each country seemed to operate differently even from each other and this concept did not change until later in the 20th century. Even the differences in the areas of the world described as the Far East, the Middle East, the continent of Africa and South America are so different from each other and the United States or North America.

When there is a careful examination of the 20th century there are so many advancements that took place. The evolution of established industries and the birth of new industries only just start to illustrate how our society and each culture were changed by these advancements. It would be unfair to state that one was more important than the other, whereas they all played a role in our evolution and development. As highlighted so many times throughout this publication, we must learn from these occurrences to learn from the past that were filled with both positive and negative events. Plus, we must use these experiences to learn for the present and most importantly for our future. If we learn from all these experiences what a wonderful world this can be, but we must take all the experiences; especially the negative events and do our best not to repeat them.

The final thought in this overview would be to list the advancements and the evolution that resulted would be equivalent to constructing a grocery or laundry list. It would be an injustice to categorize these events in such a fashion and insult all the brilliant minds that dedicated their lives to improve our society and each culture. Naturally, there is not enough room to list every advancement within the past century and there is no insult intended due to this occurrence; just human error. There are several industries that can be illustrated and convey the magnitude of advancement that took place within the last century.

As stated above, the material was carefully researched to be accurate and different than most history books published in the past. Everyone I shared this with related to me that most history books from the past was often one sided and never related the whole truth. In all truth, I was somewhat shocked by that revelation and I never expected to receive that type of critiquing from this effort. Every history book or other types of the books written always seem to be one-sided and never convey to the reader or audience the complete truth. I know that books written about the past were often slanted to support the part of the country or world it was written or published in, this was to make the country, part of the country or part of the world seem correct in their philosophy and thinking. The best example would be the reasons for the United States Civil War in the 1860's, whereas other civil wars took place for less reasons than what took place in our own civil war. Yet in the 1900's the United Nations found reasons, backed by the United States, to conducted what is deemed as police actions as the main excuse. The League of Nations, which was formed in the early 1920's after the end of World War l at the Paris Peace Conference and was dissolved in 1946. United States President Woodrow Wilson was credited to being one of the founders and at one time it consisted of 63 countries as members. It did at first only had the Allies and Neutral countries at its inception, but that grew then dwindled at the brink of World War ll in the 1930's.

The United Nations formed after World War ll in late 1945 in an effort to help maintain peace after the war involving countries throughout the world. The theory behind the formation of such an organization was to solve disagreements, problems and issues before these scenarios escalate the world into another world war. Since its inception as stated above it really achieved moderate success and the proof of this fact are the occurrence of several wars throughout the world since its inception. The results of this formation consist of mixed reviews of what real the success achieved as seen throughout the world. Questions of the success, which should be studied and examined. Like anything else exposed and displayed on the world stage, the truthful answer may be very difficult to attain. Plus, whether the answer is positive or negative may also hard to discover.

A very important point to ponder was that group of nations formed in 1949 called NATO, defined as North Atlantic Treaty Organization. This grew from 12 countries at its inception to 29 countries in North America and Europe. The question that must be honestly answered is; are these world organizations truly working and there must be a clear cut and honest agenda put in place to monitor and in sport's analogy the goal is to keep an honest scorecard. As we learned from past efforts good attentions is only half the battle, whereas follow through and results is the ultimate and only true benchmark.

Initially, the goal of all three organizations was to keep and maintain peace throughout the world through the means of communication when problems and issues took place between countries. What may seem to be ironic is that all three organizations were formed after major wars ended and peace was restored by force. The old adage of letting the horse out of the barn after it burned down seems to describe the formation and effectiveness of all three organizations. To illustrate that they were total failures would also be inaccurate, but like any other organization or venture there must be integrity by the individuals involved. To achieve peace, one must truly want it in order to maintain it and have longevity. There have been different organizations developed by the United Nations throughout the years to address different problems and issues that arose in the aftermath of some devastating events that took place in different parts of the world.

The concept and truth about the United Nations is not all bad or useless in our society and world. The organization has tried to put some programs in place just as its predecessor the League of Nations to try to improve life. Some of these programs include the United Nations of Drugs and Crime, the Organization of Community, Continuing Education, the Food and Agriculture Organization, the International Atomic Energy Agency, the Developmental Program to Eradicate Poverty and several other Programs or Agencies to improve the human condition.

Pictures of the Egyptian Sphinx and Pyramid built thousands of years ago

Chapter 2

The Beginning

If one truly examines and studies the advancements of humanity in the 20th century; it is an amazing era unlike any other time in history. A careful look at the time span between advancements seems and does get longer in nearly every era that is studied, researched and examined. The only real exception is the era of the 20th century. The 100 years termed for this purpose is the ten decades that encompasses from 1900 to 2000. The fact that the time frame that humanity has been in recorded history and in existence seems to be always changing due to new discoveries, with science trying to date or theorize when these items occurred or put a time frame when these discoveries were actually invented. What are really unexplained are some experts believe that these discoveries date further back in time than originally theorized and perhaps more developed than originally thought. Some experts believe the same discoveries predate the earliest known documentation of the existence of humanity, which includes the Old Testament of the Holy Bible, the Dead Sea Scrolls, and other documentation of early civilizations and cultures dating back over 5000BC. There may be some issues with some of these discoveries even predating the Ancient Sumerian Civilization, which is theorized to be the first civilization that occupied parts of now Iraq, Babylonia and the surrounding areas. There are now some experts who claim civilization started in the region today known as Turkey also there is some question about gauging time by the ice caps, which was a long standing- theory. This, however, does not explain the fate of the Ancient Sumerians.

The people of that civilization just seemed to have totally disappeared or became parts of other early civilizations and to this day experts theorize and debate what really happened. All that is really left are archaeological discoveries such as tools, abstract items and other forms of art of what the world and galaxy possibly looked like during that era of history. What might seem interesting is their art forms depicting our galaxy and solar system. The depiction of more than nine planets does seem interesting, considering that they really had no technology to look or see what the solar system truly consisted of apart from the obvious like the sun, our moon, the stars and perhaps some isolated other planets. Research shows the theories over the years and centuries are as numerous and infinite as the number of experts.

Pictures of the Mayan Calendar and the Pyramid

The Roman Colosseum built in 100 AD

Then comes the marvels still standing built in Ancient Egypt called pyramids and structures, which are standing today, literally thousands of years later. Within all the advancements and technology established in the past century, no one can match the ingenuity on how these structures were built. Yet to state that the Egyptians were alone in this technology would be a falsehood, whereas the structures built by the Romans still standing in Italy and the Ancient Mayans built that fantastic calendar pyramid among other structures. All these civilizations were years and literally a half a world apart. We in the so-called modern era have trouble with our buildings and structures lasting within 50 to 100 years, yet alone having them last centuries. There is constant maintenance on landmarks standing in the United States; for examples the Statue of Liberty, the Empire State Building, the Washington Monument and Lincoln Memorial, Mount Rushmore and so many other famous landmarks.

To further illustrate why the 20th century is so fascinating in human history, consider that some experts believe and theorize that humanity started developing 200,000 years ago. This was roughly estimated 64 million years after the last known species of dinosaurs. The time estimated of human development alone as we know it was estimated about 30 thousand years ago, utilizing agriculture approximately 8000BC and writings dating back roughly 3500 to 5000 BC. Naturally, different interpretations of these writings varied, but one interesting interpretation is that they might be of marriage records. The examination of these advancements was lengthy in the scope of time between each, but that seem to change as humanity became more advanced and along with technology changed the gap between advancements.

The growth or advancements, which engulfed our society locally, nationally and globally were a complete phenomenon. The changes between 1900 to 2000 AD are both astronomically and unbelievable in comparison to any age in humanity. To point out one person for this would be both unreasonable and unfair. The list of individuals in all fields shared his/her own contribution(s), which undoubtedly shaped our lives in the 20th century and beyond. The slogan or adage used so many times in both illustrates to follow and beyond documenting the

20th century is really an understatement. It is "Necessity is the Mother of Invention."

The fact that there several brilliant minds in the 20th century would be an enormous understatement. The list goes beyond Albert Einstein, Sam Walton, Bill Gates, Sears, Macy and Gimbals. As stated the list of brilliant minds are almost endless and one can write a novel size book or publication high lighting their genius and contributions shaping the 20th century and the future. The individuals listed above cannot begin the insight of brilliant individuals seemingly in almost every industry that had the talent and the ability to dream that will forever change our future on a global scale. These are just a short list of brilliant individuals, who enhanced their industries and their true brilliance was yet to be truly realized in the present generation and the future generations yet to come.

There will be a conscious effort and level to keep this as objective as possible as the study of each industry's influence is documented and evaluated from factual data and results. The only subjective levels revolve around Albert Einstein, God and Religion. Einstein, who was one of the most brilliant minds of the 20th century. He was years and decades ahead of his time. His theories about gravitational waves are only now being scientifically proven. We would be remiss if we did not include another of his famous quotes, that is "two things are infinite, the universe and human stupidity; and I'm sure about the former." He was approaching his 40's in 1916 and perhaps he could have imagined what the 20th century would influence our world in the 21st century. Keep in mind that he passed away in April 1955 and one can almost hear him whispering 'that each industry had its own brilliant minds and it should be measured by the contributions.' It is difficult to believe that he passed over 61 years ago and yet still the full impact of his brilliance and contributions are yet to be fully realized and/or fully proven. The last 45 years really created the measuring stick that really measured the true growth within the last part of the century. This truly measured the advancements that can be truly used as a true gauge of the magnitude of such changes and how life changed on every level in the 20th century in our cultural and global present and beyond.

The Washington Monument and Lincoln Memorial/ with the White House

Chapter 3

Culture

Most are quick to point out and illustrate all the positive results from the advancements in the 20th century and it would be foolish and ignorant to deny that these positive results were felt on a global scale. The change of the over-all quality of life would not be difficult to acknowledge and given the credit it truly deserves on every positive result from such changes. Each aspect deserves to be recognized, as every culture has benefited beyond all dreams and expectations. The century started with the use of cannonballs and ended with most countries amid establishing or having nuclear capability. Just as anything else, event or age in history whether it occurred within 100 years or 2000 years ago, there are consequences and results that should be a learning experience for everyone present and more importantly for the future. If the past taught us anything, the theme which cannot be stated enough, which is that history does repeat itself. Perhaps only a select few knows or knew how close that we came to devastation or complete extinction as an entire race. Nuclear capability can be used for advancements, but through accidents in different parts of the world, we have witnessed its destructive devastation.

Although there have been numerous significant advancements, the problems and issues that plagued humanity since our birth has really stayed the same and in some examples advanced and magnified in countries and cultures throughout the globe. The disturbing facts are that these circumstances have grown to a global scale, with no immunity to the negative results witnessed in nearly every part of the world. One would think with our society advancing becoming more civilized, but the sad reality is despite all these advancements and changes in the 20th century seemed to make the world a much smaller place, which really did not solve problems between countries and different issues that now exist on a global scale.

The old, but true adage, that history repeating itself never held truer than the events that have taken place in the world in the 20th century. The magnitude and magnification of these advancements in the world are really finally realized and if one really examines the entire truths, these events would be well documented on several levels. Within our history one cannot deny how truly advanced and this era or period is really unparalleled to any other time/ages in our history. However, one cannot deny that there have been the barbaric negative results that are arguably the most substantial century in human history.

We learned as time elapsed that the reality of the possibility of a 3rd World War in the 1960's was a real possibility and whether it was an interference of a Supreme Being, just a communicative error or what was learned a disobedience of orders discovered years later; that sad and devastating event almost took place. That reality only everyone can imagine how it would have shaped the present times and our future as we term as today.

The population were separated on a national or global would witness growth well beyond their imagination and dreams. Even people who were born halfway and beyond what can be considered halfway in the 20th century can be amazed in the growth and advancement that took place over the next 50 years. Witnessing the changes in nearly a 40-year time frame one cannot come close to describing how our world and society has grown on every level; without truly giving the true praise and justice that it truly deserves. This praise must include were not limited with technology only, but it must include every level of industry.

Most businesses, markets, industries (old and new) and other establishments were privately owned and carried merchandise and goods that were first a need, then wanted for its isolated and specialized population. The needs and wants for that population was dictated by geographical locations. These needs and wants were determined by the type of business in each selected geographical location. There were needs that were very common and in the same respect very different. For an example, the needs in areas where the main business or production were farming and agriculture were far different from the needs necessary for mining. Yet even the industries listed above differed in needs and wants depended on product and merchandise developed by other industries, which the population of different locations would also purchase the finished item. Economics was of utmost importance, which caused problems and issues in countries internally,

The very same could be illustrated about the United States Civil War, which took place in the 19th century. The rallying cry or reason for that war or conflict was equal rights; concerning the rights of Afro-Americans versus the rights of European Americans. Several history books and documentations of that war conveniently omitted that there were other reasons; most glaring is or was economics and separation of the country. This war or action took place in pre-20th century; naturally even historians argue or debate the reason for this war to this very day. The main transportation was limited to travel by foot, horseback or train in certain developed areas of the United States and the world. Even Henry Ford's idea of the horseless carriage form of travel known as a car or public transportation known as travel for public use was a far-off dream and eventually turned into reality decades later at best. It is important to understand that the idea of the automobile was not Ford's idea originally as others throughout history tried different energy sources for the mechanism. None were really successful until the use of gasoline powered mechanisms was introduced and Ford's brilliance came in mass producing it as described in this chapter. As history showed in any human age or era; the use of all advancements was used by the government or military first, whether domestic or foreign. Once again, the ever-popular terminology was widely used; once again for national security. This seems to be a reoccurring theme as the history of the 20th century continues through the decades.

There was no time or era like the 20th century, where the entire globe was going to change and advance unlike any time in human history. Changes have always been part of human history, but no one could ever predict the gravity of changes or more amazing the quality and difference of life between 1900 and 2000. The best illustration to show this analogy is the comparison of how large the world seemed in 1900. There was no air travel and technology was very limited. The eventual growth of technology such as air travel and as noted above the emergence of the automobile industry played a major role in growth and advancement. It is important to note that each industry had growth and influence in life of the 20th century. One can only imagine considering the night sky, seeing the moon and within seventy years our society would put people on that very same moon; for sure it would be categorized as beyond science fiction at the start of the century. Analog and digital electronics were not established at that point, where the tubes and picture taken were still relatively in its infancy.

Even the concept of the horseless carriage, eventually called the automobile, was still in the developmental stage. Henry Ford's idea of mass production of the automobile was still in its infancy; naturally companies like General Motors and other auto producing companies eventually followed. The idea formulated by Wilbur and Orville Wright with plane travel eventually took hold and developed beyond anyone's dreams. These were only a few examples of the brilliant minds yet to follow in what can be termed as the 20th century.

One cannot really illustrate how industries influenced other industries in the 20th century and beyond without documenting the evil events, which led to some sad and devastating results. The familiar concept of wars over the equally familiar reasons of religion, economics and real estate has been a constant theme since the birth of humanity to even today. Within this advancement in almost every industry and the before mentioned birth of some new industries came with more efficient ways to destroy and kill. There have been some suggestion using several mediums stating that 'The Holocaust in Nazi, Germany never happened. This would be a total falsehood and a complete lie, a total denial of true human history. That would be like stating Pearl Harbor, the destruction of the European Continent in two World Wars and the use of the atom bomb on Hiroshima and Nagasaki, Japan never took place. There are several reminders throughout the world that these barbaric and uncivilized events did indeed take place. In North

America, all anyone should do is visit Arlington Cemetery or visit Pearl Harbor, Hawaii for a reality check. One can only imagine the loss of all those brilliant minds and the unforgivable waste of the taking of human lives. If there needs to be further convincing, all one only should visit certain areas of both Germany and Japan, where there are reminders still standing today (over 70 years later). Yet the taking of human life is a true tragic constant today as it was in the history of humanity.

To finish the recap of the 20th century, one would be remiss not to include the Korean War, the Viet Nam Conflict, nuclear capability and terrorism. The first two items on this list were civil wars, which the United States involved the military under the guise of United Nations sanctioned actions. The Korean War was properly named, but in the case of the Viet Nam Conflict there is some confusion with the terminology. Anytime someone or a group of people are holding military automatic weapons at each other and shooting them, that is called a war. It must be a major issue with families, who lost love ones in such an engagement. Fighting a bully on your neighborhood street is a conflict, whereas the Viet Nam conflict should be renamed to its original name, The Viet Nam War.

The next to last subject on the list is nuclear capability, which was used to replace the use of the atom. Reactors were set up in both countries first termed as the super powers, which would include the United States and Russia. The first objective was to replace the atom bomb and use nuclear energy as weapons. As the century evolved the idea shifted to use nuclear capability as a form of energy in strategic parts of each country. The accident at Chernobyl, Russia illustrated the devastation that it can cause and both countries seem to unilaterally agree to decrease the weapon use of nuclear energy. The affects in Russia are still being felt to this very day and both sides seem to agree to decrease nuclear weaponry over a set period. These agreements were set up in accordance to the United Nations accord achieved through diplomatic channels. The devastation in Russia is only an example what nuclear weaponry use can be established and it is important to note that this took place accidental. Whether both sides to abide honorably to the decrease of weaponry capability can only be determined over an elapse period of time. Once again, the only result can be determined over a period and whether both sides act responsibly in using such an unstable element.

The last subject on the list mentioned above is terrorism. These are acts of violence either committed by a group or country for fanatical or religious reasons. It does mirror actions done by the Catholic Church in the Middle Ages. For whatever reasons, it is done makes it wrong and barbaric. The excuses for the Catholic Church are at least these senseless acts happened centuries ago, whereas groups like Isis and alike can offer no real excuses except that different people call and worship God differently. With all the advancements, where is the sense in that thinking? What Supreme Being would deem it necessary to kill other human beings? Surely, it would not be a supreme being worth worshiping and one would think that there may be some confusion at best or the works of the evil one. The truth is that such actions have been taken place throughout the history of humanity, even before the first written word was ever recorded.

Chapter 4

Philosophy and Economics

The beginning of any era whether it is the history of the 20th century or the existence of the so-called intelligent life forms depicted as human beings. In all reality religion is an essential part of the past, present and future, but there will be an effort to limit somewhat the bringing of the subject of religion or beliefs into the study of influential industries that helped shape our lives nationally in the United States and eventually globally throughout every so-called civilization or country now in existence. Also included is any country or group that gave its birth in the last 20 years of the 20th century.

Naturally, like any law or rule established by us human beings, there are always exceptions built in and this is no exception. To quote the Holy Bible specifically the most controversial and least understood, the gospel accordingly by John; "In the beginning there was the Word; from that came the Law from Moses, but Truth and Grace came from Jesus Christ." The only reason to mention this especially after the opening paragraph is the fact there are over 1.2 billion Catholics in the world. Along with this fact plus the members of other Christian faiths, which were influenced by a so-called man's three- year ministry that by all accounts was something very special. All he preached was love and peace, which is something special even in today's standards.

Choosing the subject content or industries that influenced or contributed to our current society would be difficult without including philosophy. These industries include those that were well established and new industries to address both the needs and wants of a growing population. To this point in human history many advancements were developed to address a need or want of a certain geographical area or location, but as the century progressed, industries were created by these advancements to address something new and very much on the horizon. The issues of a growing global population and the essentials because of such growth. The fact and what may be hard to imagine the age of this planet and thinking about how long humanity evolved in comparison to that time frame. This time comparison of the existence of humanity in comparison to other life cycles of everything that took place on this planet is a blink of an eye when science is considering all the other life forms and cycles that took place in this world or third planet in this solar system that we call home.

It is difficult to keep in mind that in the year 1900, we as both a country and society in the United States were only 35 years removed from the civil war and the Lincoln assassination. We also as a civilization almost pushed a race of people to extinction; the American Indian. It may be difficult to keep mindful, but it is important to note that we are describing a century that had issues and problems. A careful examination would show a documentation of two World Wars, several other smaller wars; including civil wars and so-called conflicts, finally concluding with terrorism and a reversal of the philosophy of religious freedom and practices on a global scale. The horror is this took place on a global scale and the prejudice regarding race, color, creed, sex, what name you called God and how that God was worshiped; along with other issues plagued our society in the 20th century since our inception. The fact of the familiar issues still revolved around Religion, Real Estate and Economics.

If one would really think about and study the emergence of the 20th century, one would discover that most countries; especially the United States would be classified as isolationists. Most countries throughout the world were either in its infancy or dealing with issues and problems within its own borders. The formation of such governing bodies like the League of Nations and its successors the United Nations were established after some event like worldwide war that took place. These worldwide organizations wielded no real power, but were established during peacetime to monitor like its predecessor for a host of reasons. The main reasons were to improve communication on a worldwide basis and to ensure peace treaties between countries at war that encompassed both World Wars for both sides, but for all countries in that era. The most important reason to establish this monitoring forum that all involved was to established peace treaties for all countries at war that encompassed for both world wars, but also for countries in that era. The fact that the most important reason to established that all involved and on a global scale would avoid the same issues and problems that resulted the world at war and on a global scale, insomuch all involved engaged and still resulted two world wars. These problems and issues could have resolved and avoided the world from engagement in two world wars, it was created to keep the world from war and solve problems with issues during peacetime. In theory behind this idea was put in place to monitor disagreements between countries and keep them from escalating tensions to avoid wars and so-called conflicts. The concept has only been partially effective at best, since there have been wars in almost every decade the United Nations has been in existence. In theories and practices, it was supposed to be a peace keeping tool used by all nations and yet the United Nations have sanctioned wars, so-called conflicts and police actions in different parts of the world. Then add terrorism to the mix, we have a society lost in confusion. If one is truly honest philosophically globally and the population was lost in confusion especially after World War I, which was referred as 'The Great War' before other wars were being numbered or named specific wars or so-called conflicts.

As illustrated above along with religion, real estate and economics seem to be the familiar rallying cry, theme and reasons for such actions not only throughout the entire past, the 20th century and right up to our present throughout the entire world. It is time for the entire world to take ownership of these issues and stop all the senseless actions of a few or the minority just wanting to play god.

The Economics

The realization that the 20th century went through several changes economically as it did in terms as advancements. The fact that the century began with farming and agriculture is an undeniable truth. In the start of the century the largest industry was the railroad, but that soon was replaced by the births of other industries. The past mode of shipping import and export of goods and merchandise became more efficient as the century progressed. The birth of the airplane and other types of transportation became commonplace throughout the world and the United States to help contribute to this efficiency.

The economy in the United States witnessed the great prosperity of 'the Roaring 1920's to the devastation of the Great Depression in the 1930's. The aftermath of two World Wars with several other wars in virtually every country in the world. The sad reality that these wars were good for business despite the murderous actions of countries, regimes and tyrants against innocent men, women and children. The real benchmark can be witnessed as early as 1945 in Germany, where there was a concerted effort to eliminate a whole race of people. To state that was just an isolated case or incident would be a falsehood as world events illustrates that other regimes, radicals and dictators are engaging in murderous activity right up to the present time. What seems to be remarkable are the efforts of these tyrants and their allies to justify what can only be labelled as the loss of human lives.

There was another economic boom in the 1950's, which can be best illustrated by the evolution of radio, the birth of television and the continually growth of the movie industry. To mention just these three components would be an injustice to all the other industries maturing and evolving. It would not be an understatement that almost every industry had organizations testing the boundaries of the Sherman Anti-Trust Law, which was established in the United States to keep organizations from monopolizing in a particular-market. In fact, one of the most recent cases was brought up against Bill Gates and Microsoft, although Mr. Gates is also involved in several humanitarian projects.

The 1960's started with what was referred to as Camelot and although the economy looked sound; it would be marred by three significant assassinations of leaders of the decade. This included President John F. Kennedy, Activist Martin Luther King and most likely a possible future President, Robert F. Kennedy. Although there were violence and murders that marred the decade, the 1960's seem to be sound. Although some experts claim that the age of certainty came to an end. The violence created economic confusion at best, with most questioning leadership issues and problems especially in the United States. It is however can be known as the decade of the end of certainty. The prime example of this lack of certainty could be the inept study of the murder of John F. Kennedy conducted by the Warren Commission.

The 1970's initially offered new hope until corruption high in the government, especially with the conviction of the United States Vice President Spiro Agnew and the eventually the Resignation of then President Richard Nixon for is involvement in infamous Watergate break-in and eventually cover-up. Adding a crisis surrounding fossil fuel, thus creating the first real issues about the economy surrounding a commodity being imported into the United States. The country ended up electing a Peanut farmer for President and ended up electing an old actor as President to finish the decade and starting the new decade; the1980's

Most experts claim that the 1980's was the decade of the start of excessive spending and the start of the debt issue. This might have been the beginning, but there is no ignoring the fact that the United States' National Debt is approaching 20 trillion dollars with no sign of slowing down in 2017. The World's Debt is also showing no signs of slowing down. The old movie actor tried pushing the concept of Reganomics to solve the debt issue. The concentration on the defense in the United States to include the Strategic Defense Initiative, which was nick named Star Wars. The focus of economics seemed to be sidetracked in the name of Defense and National Security.

The 1990's was deemed the era by most experts the return of the United States economy starting in 1995 and booming in 1999. This revival was short lived as corporations started to send jobs overseas or out of the country. Such initiatives like NAFTA helped realize the benefit of using cheaper labor, thus diminishing the job market within the borders of the United States. Although there was a short-term success, but the result would do damage to the middle class. The future terminology of the U.S. label and made in the United States was the theme in the early 21st century.

One cannot ignore the outrageous World and United States' Debt Clock. Reaching into the multiple trillions for numerous countries, which reaches far beyond irresponsible spending. The movie the first Exorcist was termed as the scariest movie ever made until anyone with any commonsense sees the World's and the United States' Debt Clock. It reflects more horror and at best a questionable economic future. The answer is far beyond the concept of a family, business, state, country or world spending far more than revenues and taxes from the inhabitants and citizen base.

The methods of advertisement have forever changed what would be defined in an expanding market share and an organization's ability to reach potential consumers. Although the Sunday paper was still being utilized, there were new avenues to create product awareness and develop an organization's ability to fill a need, to fill an illusion of a need and to fill a want. The last forty years revolved around evolution to improve market shares to a global scale. The bottom line was the 20th century may have started as a world engulfed in farming, agricultural and in midst of an industrial revolution, but it evolved beyond nearly everyone's imagination to 24-a-day shopping and the information age. Also, the concept that advertisement is done on a personal level, whereas each campaign is geared to the individual's shopping habits and preference. The practice of the outdated retail chain of inventor/ manufacturer to wholesaler/ distributer to retailer to finally the customer seems destined for the history books.

The short overview of economics in the 20th century does not begin to cover the changes that each decade brought to the United States and the world. Colleges and Universities offer four to eight-year programs that highlight the depressions, recessions, inflations, stock market occurrences, world wars, civil wars, so-called police actions, small wars, conflicts, terrorism and other economic scenarios that took place. The future does not offer or paint anything that would offer relief economically. This especially holds true with countries like North Korea and China more interested in building their military, acquiring

Real Estate and devoting so much money to their nuclear weaponery. The bold question must be asked, how many missiles or bombs does it take to blow ourselves up; thus making the human race extinct? Most experts estimate that the world's population will grow to over 11 billion by 2100. The challenge to our world leaders today is to put all these selfish petti issues aside and concentrate to collectively to fix our world's economy for the sake of one 'Race' we all belong to called, 'The Human Race' and for our grandchildren's children; the future.

Throughout the history of humanity, the world has witnessed every form of government. Whether we examine or study democracy, socialism, communism, republic, dictatorship or any other form or combination listed, governments still have economic problems and issues in the result. There does not seem to be a clear answer to solve these problems and issues. Some idealists and dreamers may suggest the impossible as listed above, whereas the countries of the world become as civilized as our advancements to the economic hardships is the entire world's problem.

Chapter 5

The Medical Field

If there is any industry that truly measures and illustrates the advancement of the 20th century without any question the medical field is really the benchmark. The medical field advanced and change so much in the century, insomuch that at the start of the century physicians were still utilizing leeches to bleed their patients; in the belief, this method would cure diseases and the release of bad toxins. As the century progressed specialized fields such as Pediatrics, Geriatrics, OBGYN, Orthopedics, Hematology, Cardiac and other specialties were established. The treatment options also developed and some examples include vaccines, surgical procedures (orthopedic, organ transplants, dialysis, laser nuclear medicine and the list seems endless) Although the century has been filled with epidemics, pandemics and other life taking diseases such as cancer, polio, tuberculosis, aids, etc. The cures and treatments for long established health issues plaguing humanity far outnumber the health problems and issues listed above. It seems like the world was plagued with diseases, the evolution of new influenza and other issues plus what can be termed as orphan diseases and other health problems plaguing the planet that certainly affected the population's mortality, whereas life expectancy were much shorter for the population in the immediate past. The best example of orphan disease would be in the category of ALS or Lou Gehrig Disease. Sadly, this was defined that not enough of the population suffered from the ailment, so it was in all truth ignored by the medical industry. Even these health problems and issues took place in United States, where medical care was much more advanced than lesser developed countries throughout the world.

The concept of Emergency Rooms in hospitals was somewhat a novelty, just as being seen by a doctor in an office setting with treatment rooms was not yet commonplace until our society progressed further into the century. This did not necessarily mean that doctors did not have offices to treat their patients. In patient care it would often depend on the type of illness, injury, etc. and how the individual doctor ran his or her practice. Other issues would include geographical location and the availability of transportation; these factors, along with others (age, sex, etc.) would determine whether doctors made house calls. This was mostly utilized at the start of the century until around the mid 1900's, then doctors in more populated areas would set-up offices to practice and treat their patients. The medical field had clinics as most illnesses and diseases, plus the treatments were basically new and treatment methods were experimental in most cases. Plus, the fact illnesses and diseases were classified in the orphan stage such as the mentioned ALS or Lou Gehrig Disease, smallpox, etc. Treatments for such were unknown like cancer.

Some outrageous population control enthusiastic groups would use this concept to control the population on a worldwide basis, which would seem outrageous to many of the population that have common sense, human decency and very much goes against the reason or theme behind medical care or the profession. The very concept of medical treatment would be the opposite of that very concept. The old substandard of biting on a bullet or drinking bourbon or some other liquor was the normal procedure for most medical procedures, which included surgeries prior to anesthetic medications and compounds discovered in the early part of the 20th century to keep the patient somewhat pain free before, during and after the procedure performed by medical surgeons. The medical field was very slow in its evolution throughout most of the history of humanity until the first part of the 20th century.

The advancements and the exciting prospects of the medical field offered several new ways to extend and save lives for the population never witnessed or experienced before in human history. The practice of medicine became a profession that was constantly evolving and was becoming more available to the population that would eventually grow to a global scale. To state or claim that there was no medical care available totally would be a falsehood. The history of the profession dates back for centuries, but a clear understanding of the scientific workings of the human body were unclear to most that practiced the profession before the 20th century. Several of the plagues that took place in the middle ages and prior were linked to sanitation issues or problems within towns and areas that were well populated. Some medical professionals in that era throughout history started to link the problem of sanitation to most plagues and diseases. Surprisingly a doctor not really linked to the medical profession, but historically famous for other reasons, named Nostradamus, was in high demand because he was highly successful in treating one of the worse plagues in European history. This literally took place centuries before the 20th century and well documented in several histories in not only France, his native country, but throughout the European continent.

Like any other advancements throughout human history, the evolution of the medical industry was a very slow evolution until the 20th century. There were brilliant minds before the 20th century, but they were far and well scattered in each culture. As illustrated in other fields, there were no shortage of advancements in the medical industry. There were issues and problems initiated by different sources that seem to slow the progress down as it did in any scientific related field or industry. This was really started by the Catholic Church in the Middle Ages, whereas anything scientifically unexplained was a product from God. There was a period in history that science was not recognized and anyone who opposed that view by the Catholic Church was dealt with in the harsher way, which meant prison or death.

Significant advancements occurred throughout the century, but the real improvements to prolong life took place in the last twenty years of the century. The concepts such as organ transplants and other specialized medical procedures became commonplace within the medical industry than any other period in human history. Most conditions, which would be classified as incurable or a certain death sentence suddenly changed to treatable. The medical industry was in midst of changing to the age of the specialist separated by the illness, disease and which part of the body was in peril. There was and is a necessity for primary care physicians, but in essence they referred patients to specific specialist for each ailment in question. Some common illnesses were cancer, smallpox, influenza, ALS and tuberculosis to name just a few and this type of practice was unheard of in the immediate past, which would include this concept up to twenty or thirty years previously.

Illustrated above the medical filed has gone through a dramatic shift as far as treatments for different diseases and illnesses to the point where some have literally disappeared off the face of the earth except in less developed countries. These have been eradicated by different treatment options that include medications and vaccines. The truth and honest fact is the mortality, success of treatment in the long term can be best be described as very slim in most cases that can be classified as medical miracles. Often these cases were terminal and classified as death sentences in much of these very same illnesses and diseases at the initial stage of diagnosis. Physicians were unable to give these patients not even the slightest chance of hope. Since the last part of the 20th century there has been a radical change unlike any other time or era in the history of humanity.

There were a host of advancements and changes in the ladder part of the century. Most likely was the ability of the medical industry's ability to prolong life by the ability to perform transplants involving the heart, kidney and other major organs. The essential facts are such transplants were in the planning stages in the past in virtually decades' prior the act of such procedures would be classified as science fiction.

Chapter 6

Newspapers/Notices

This form of communication can be dated back at least as far back in the history of humanity when the earliest form of written communication was documented between 3500 to 5000BC. There are some experts that date it back further than that period through and due to the discoveries of art, which are from different civilizations and cultures throughout the world, which seems to question the accuracy of the above dating. What seems to be remarkable are the distances in terms of where on the planet each civilization existed and developed; especially without the modes of transportation established roughly only 100 years ago. This medium would be used for centuries announcing upcoming events much like the list of events of what might take place in the ancient Roman Coliseum and in cultures or civilizations before and after that era in human history. These structures would house all forms of entertainment for the citizens and other people in attendance for these events. There would be officials in charge of posting notices of these events to insure proper and maximum attendance. It would be a falsehood to state that all the events that took place in these complexes were ethically and morally right. In fact, there were competitions between men referred to as gladiators, including battles against wild animals with gladiators or innocent men, women or children or wild animals battling each other. The result would mean death for any of the losers of such competitions, which would be posted on the outside walls like a modern sports score along with the next day's or future upcoming events. It seems that each civilization and culture had its own communication system. What seems clear is that each had its own method and language for such systems throughout human history. What seems remarkable and unique is that each civilization also developed its own unique languages.

To convey the fact that that there was no written word until the newspaper became available to the population would be false, because it was both a critical essential and an important key throughout the advancements in history. Just as any other advancement in humanity. What holds true with any advancement whether it occurred manipulating nature, the combination of science and nature or just scientifically alone there was an evolution in the growth process.

It would be wrong if the fact was omitted that the telegraph was indeed developed in the 19th century and a very popular form of communication over long distances. This would only be possible through putting up what later became known as telephone poles and hanging a wire from each outpost to outpost; normally the facility would be a train station or post office. The use of Morse code was most likely the most popular way to send messages or news using the telegraph. Although it was useful in the conveyance of messages and news, it was somewhat unreliable because of the use of wires were above ground. It would be subject to wires being cut between each facility or designated receiving office through natural or other means.

The first real form of public advertisement or communications tool was the newspaper utilized by most retailers, other businesses, companies or organized reporting agencies used this form of communication to inform the public first locally and then revolved in most respects as the public grew on a much wider basis. As the population really increased not only nationally, but globally as well, the newspaper or a more elaborated advertisement tool was utilized by most government agencies, organizations, businesses and companies to announce news, sales and advertisements. The newspapers also informed the public of local, national and world events, which were highlighted mainly in the Sunday's publications unless the country was in the midst of war (IE major news or events like World Wars). Most of the newspapers were local at best, because of the distribution issues at its initial birth. Normally, it was largest on Sunday's and it would contain advertisements and news that would contain news and advertisements for the local retailers, other businesses and local news makers representing various industries in the immediate area, including government news. This medium would also include news worthy events that as before mentioned in all venues including local, state, national and international venues that has taken place.

For a long period of time in the history of humanity a form of the newspaper was the only avenue of communication on nearly every level, whether it was authored by the leadership of the country, leadership of the church in power (for centuries in the middle ages it was the Catholic Church), notifying the public of unofficial and official news and any other form of communication. As stated above writings can be dated back to almost 5000 BC and it changed or evolved to different methods as humanity advanced through the centuries. What may seem to be amazing that different cultures in some cases totally separated from each other, in some cases literally half a world apart from each other, developed their own unique alphabet and ways to document their own communication methods.

Within the 20th century there were several types of communication methods, but to document that entire process was established in that time frame would be untrue and false. One, however, cannot deny the evolution of the process to different formats and how each changed our society and culture in every way imaginable. The subject matter would include books and magazines used for education, fiction, non-fiction and science fiction publications, magazines (that would every subject imaginable for every age group and intellect), each geographical regions' newspaper (for example the New York Times, New Jersey Star Ledger, The Los Angeles Chronicle, Orlando Sentinel and several other examples). These can include examples of magazines available virtually of every activity, sport, soap opera, gossip, even sensational news and everything in between.

The essential importance of communication and each culture as illustrated above developed on their own, which is even still being debated among experts where it initially started. This is due to new discoveries, which provide art forms and the actual translation of the above-mentioned interpretations of these findings being debated by experts throughout the world. It seems that as science answer questions about our past, there are always new ones to take their place and as highlighted so many times what awaits us on the horizon. The most interesting concept of the communication question are the number of languages that were developed through the history of humanity. As mentioned above does mention communication methods that were a great geographical distance from each culture in reference to the geographical and in reference to time periods in history of each culture, but now the issue of totally different languages produces more questions and now the dating of these establish languages seem to create more questions as we advance into the future. As far for language in general, it is an essential component for communication for any culture being examined or studied.

Chapter 7

Electricity

The main thought that comes to mind when people throughout the globe think about electricity are lighting, appliances and other items that need a power source to operate and function. However, before the discovery and more importantly the use of electricity, lighting at night was the main thought of most people living in the centuries before the widespread use. The main source of lighting in that era was the use of torches or camp fires with different types of accelerant as the power source. This concept will change as the use of electricity is documented in this chapter.

When people mention the word electricity, the first thought in several minds cannot help associating this to lighting. As the examination of the discovery or term known as electricity really means so much more especially in the 20th century and the inventions that led to so many advancements since its discovery. It is really linked in so many advancements as the century progressed and how it changed the society or humanity since its discovery, which include the quality of life in so many countries across the globe. Actually, a very little known fact is that the Greeks discovered a form of electricity about 2600 years ago (around 600 BC), although there was no real use of it until much later in history. The discovery was the facts of static energy, which was known as electricity that did not move. Roughly around 2200 years later an English physicist named William Gilbert wrote books about amber and the Latin term electricus, which described the effects. Years later Thomas Browne, inspired by Gilbert, wrote books about the findings, which the term of electricity was finally used. Benjamin Franklin in 1752 did his famous experiments with the kite and key, but he was not the man who officially discovered electricity.

Other scientists and doctors discovered electricity through different experiments that yield some different results and advancements. Some examples included an Italian doctor in 1800 named Luigi Galvani did experiments with frogs, insomuch the frog's legs would twitch touching two metals establishing an electrical charge. From this result Allessandro Volta found that electricity can exhibit a steady flow, which was not necessarily sudden or violent. It was the establishment of the flow of electrical charge. This produced the idea for the initial battery, which included AAA (1.5 volts) and other types of batteries. Now these were primitive in comparison to the batteries of today, but these were eventually used as a power source for transistor radios and other advancements needing that type of power source in order to operate or function. Transistor radios need 9 volts and car batteries need 12 volts to operate, which came later with the advancement of the automobile.

This list seems to move forward as the scientist Michael Faraday proved that moving magnets can move an electrical charge. This not only proved the theories and the success of the experiments from the past, but it opened the door for scientists to investigate the potential of the possibility of moving electrical charge in discoveries and advancements for most importantly for the future. The next significant discover was made by Nickola Tesla. He proved that charges were capable of moving back and forth in a wire instead of only one direction. His theory and experiment proved alternate current, which will be examined and evaluated as the results of his work and experiments will be further studied of his theories will be further proven and highlighted. The next real name in the scientific community would have to include Thomas Alva Edison, who was another brilliant scientific mind, who had a theory mind concerning in direct current, which is still realized in today's world on so many levels. There has been an effort to review some important scientists, who have played a role in establishing electricity and for certain there are other brilliant scientists that contributed to this phenomenon and to mention them was purely unintentional and there is no offense meant; as there were important people not mentioned in other important influences that were also unintentional. Electricity was in its infancy towards the end of the 1800's and the famous battle of the currents involving alternate current (AC) against direct current (DC) took place in New York City after AC installations were built to accommodate the electrical needs for homes and businesses in the era.

The real debate or battle took place between Tesla and Edison before the start of the 20th century in the 1880's and 1890's. It involved Thomas Edison with General Electric against Nikola Tesla with Westinghouse, which involved two theories of electrical current. It became the war of the current that involved alternate current (Tesla) against direct current (Edison). Most established cities and other populated areas were already setup with systems for alternate current as the main energy source throughout the world. It is important to understand that there was a new era the world was embarking upon, which is the Industrial Revolution. Business leaders like J.P. Morgan, Andrew Carnegie and other industrial business leaders would put their full support behind Edison's Direct Current theory in this battle of the currents. The reason was because they already built installations for direct current in New York City. However, the city had installations for both types of systems. To take a real honest look at the so-called battle, both sides were guilty of unscrupulous acts or campaigns to point out the dangers of both current system; more so possibly towards the AC then the DC. Both sides pushed their standpoint, thus appearing more like a nasty political race during an election where both opponents would resort to underhanded tactics to make each side look bad.

Although Edison technically lost the battle, both types of installations were used as the century progressed especially in New York City. For a period of time the alternate current installations more than fit the needs. There was a period of time that both electrical current installations, alternate current and direct current, were both used, it was not really until towards the end of 1900's and the start of the 21st century when that scenario changed. This all changed because of advancements in the century would require DC energy source, these included computers, LED lights, cell phones, electrical cars and other products and equipment. DC lines were more reliable in reference to offering more capacity per line, thus reducing less blackouts, because it did not cascade faults as much as AC did and AC were costlier due to heavier lines and other factors. The DC based grids operated with smaller equipment, offered the customer better quality, it became more efficient in terms of energy, eventually was less complex than AC, led to lower cost to the customer and other factors. As stated above both power sources were being utilized throughout the century.

The 20th century was the era of human advancement and documented throughout this recap of the industries that were both discoveries and influences of not only within the century, but also for the future; how can this ever be complete without highlighting the discovery and the many uses of electricity. Although the discovery of electricity actually took place prior to the 1900's, widespread use and the potential were not fully realized until well into the 20th century. It became the main power source for several discoveries in the century and this included lights, refrigerators, radios, computers, televisions, freezers, several different types of appliances and other advancements. It changed life on several levels, which be eventually felt in the entire world with some exceptions. In almost every country throughout the world it has become the main power source for what is now as the way that is now familiar and commonplace in nearly country in the world.

This is really the study that the legitimacy of technology and what truly makes the advancements of technology reliable and realistic as our society grows in both the present market and the future market that included the population yet to be newly born in our future in the 21st century and beyond. electricity. The heartbreaking fact is that Tesla and Edison were both brilliant scientists and inventors literally years and decades ahead of their time in respect to the knowledge that improved our lives on a global scale. This was never truly realized because the scope of their brilliance and the results of their concepts were embroiled with the war of the currents until years later. This fact made their contributions unappreciated and not fully realized until several years later in respect to the industry, the population and the other educated benefactors. They realized their contributions in some rare cases that took place immediately, but years later in our developmental history, how it shaped our reality in the past and the outcome of our world today.

The evolution of electricity is not limited to sending it across wires that crisscrossed across the country and the globe. There became other ways to produce this power source through different means. The use of different means that included retrieving energy from the initial source developing different forms of batteries, discoveries by brilliant scientists (Tesla, Edison and others), large dams. atomic energy, nuclear energy, solar energy and other sources developed since its inception.

If one examines just one by-product of electricity, which would be the source of light during the evening hours, it would be illustrated that fire was the first source and utilized for several centuries. The uses went far beyond lighting, whereas fire was used for several different advancements. Eventually, an accelerant was utilized to prolong the time that the fire or light could be used in term of the different advancements and discoveries developed by humanity throughout the centuries. To convey what life consisted of a mere century ago and trying to convey life centuries, which include thousands of years ago is extremely difficult to first share with the younger generation and in the same context try to make them understand the gravity of changes. This was all due to the discovery of electricity and its many uses.

Chapter 8

Technology

The subject of technology covers everything and was really the theme of the 20th century. The definition of everything as far as technology is concerned would include any advancement or discovery developed by science to improve and enhance the quality of life. This also includes all forms of entertainment enhanced and magnified for the general population. Although black and white pictures were available to the elite and infamous in the ladder part of the 19th century, its true availability did not take place until the early part of the 20th century. This subject matter is so wide and to just list each electronic advancement in chronological order would not really do it justice. To really put you in the proper mind set, just imagine being a 16- year- old child in 1900 in comparison to being a 16- year- old child in the year 2000. Besides the before mentioned Albert Einstein, who could imagine the advancements in a mere 100 years? Going from silent movies and radio to more than 250 channels in today's household would be considered science fiction in 1900. The fact that live entertainment goes back for centuries does not relate the impact of technology to our society throughout the 20th and beginning of the 21st century. Just to illustrate just that one difference would not properly magnify and reveal the differences in the decades yet to follow.

There would be a real big error in highlighting the 20th century without illustrating the technological marvel invented by Alexander Graham Bell called the telephone. At first only the real elite of society could afford this luxury and eventually as the century progressed this technological marvel from the 19th century became the main communication tool in the United States and most of the world. It was common to see telephones in most homes and organizations among the population and to witness phone booths in businesses and street corners in most countries throughout the world. The benefits of the telephone industry were initially not truly realized until it grew with the population and was more than a communication tool used for advancement by organizations. It was an effective communication tool on every level, which included local, state, national and eventually international levels. This made it unique, insomuch up to that point in human history instant communication was not a reality.

The real truths of the 20th century cannot be truly illustrated without the facts about technology, which really influenced every advancement that took place. The brilliant minds that were in every industry would only start to touch the tip of the iceberg, so to speak. The scope and reality is now only being realized and each industry is only now starting to be acknowledged because of technology. What might be overwhelming is truly technology is still relatively young and the evolution is constantly changing, plus if used responsibly it can change lives for more positive results than negative purposes. Like everything else in our society, the use or discovery of new technologies can be used to improve the quality of our world in nearly every way imaginable or it can establish the complete opposite result. This can only happen, as history teaches us, if people use this present and new technology responsibly. It would require a true commitment towards growth that would yield positive results and improvements on a global scale.

Among all the technology advancements and discoveries in the century must involve the concept of space travel, which stemmed from air travel. The super powers of the era that included the United States and Russia initially developed programs to start space exploration that resulted traveling to our moon, thus putting a person on that body. Each country had its own space program, which expanded to a worldwide participation resulting in a space station. Eventually, within the century and in the following century there was an international space station built theoretically for all countries involved in the space programs. The space program included sending unmanned probes to other planets and bodies within our solar system. The program also sending the same probes outside the solar system to learn what is beyond our solar system and possibly answer other scientific questions. United States president John F. Kennedy in 1960 referred that space exploration was the last frontier and boldly predicted that we would put a human being on our moon within ten years, by 1970 and we accomplished the feat in 1969.

There were several other space missions to the moon and to especially develop a program by the United States and other countries to develop an international space station. This specifically developed to explore the solar system and to what may beyond the solar system. The scientific view was to explore other worlds and planets within our solar system to try to find answers to questions about earth. By finding answers about our planet, the theory is that we may find answers about our true past. Also by working together in this method the answers to questions about the moon, the sun and other planets may be answered on a quicker basis and as a world and civilization we may be able to expand more quickly outside the solar system. There are already missions using probes to study not only our solar system, outside or beyond our solar system and the development of theories on how life began.

old radio

Chapter 9

Radio

The medium of radio was and still is a very good and successful medium for advertisement, being used by almost every industry in the designated market. Companies would dedicate advertisement budgets for this use to gain more market shares in particular regions and markets. The use of popular and colorful personalities from nearly every field or industry would be utilized; for an example the use of Ty Cobb and Babe Ruth were engaged to advertise for nearly every product or merchandise line from candy bars to other lines of merchandise. The use of radio was really the first, which we will term, as an electronic form of promotion of merchandise used by organizations to advertise to particular populations to individual markets. Radio use, initially were far different than the ones used as the century progressed. Keep in mind that these radios were operated by the initial stages of analog electronics with batteries as the main power source. Electricity was really still in its infancy and widespread use was only in the beginning stages and the availability was somewhat limited and isolated because of geographical locations.

These popular personalities in our culture were not the only tools used to advertise for a company or product line. Popular personalities from movies; for an example actors and actresses like William Powell and Myrna Loy would not only perform on this medium as the characters that they acted in movies, whereas they would also advertise a diverse line of products and merchandise from several companies in various industries. They would serve as sponsors for such programming and advertise heavily to a target audience in the population. Radio was not just limited to music, insomuch development of various programming included westerns, glamorizing the gangsters of the era, detective shows and even comic book super heroes and characters plus science fiction formats were eventually utilized. Often these half hour programs would dedicate nearly half of the air time to advertisement. As illustrated above these programs would target specific parts of the population or market.

At one point in the 20th century it was the best and only form of electronic entertainment for most of the population apart from the evolution of movies. The radio audience only consisted of the poor and rich class. The real emergence of the middle did not take place until later in the century. This was basically due to advancements of some already established industries and the birth of new industries as the century progressed. As stated earlier, radio was a great medium of entertainment, for instance it would involve everything from sports and nearly all phases of fiction and non-fiction programming. This would include science fiction, which really took hold in the 1950's, and news to keep the population informed about local, national and international events, Franklin Delano Roosevelt, who was president of the United States from 1933 to 1945, used the medium of radio to talk to the country in his famous 'Fireside Chats.' The use of this medium was brilliant on several levels; especially for both political and popularity reasons. Nothing illustrates Franklin D, Roosevelt's popularity more than the fact that he was the only United States president elected to four terms in office and held that position or office until he passed away in 1945. It is important to note that congress voted to limit the consecutive terms of the office to two consecutive 4- year terms.

The fact and reality that if Franklin D. Roosevelt had access to the medium or tool of television; given the mindset of the average voter in the 1930's and 1940's; the question that is asked if he would have been elected to even one term as president yet alone to four terms? In concert with news and political purposes, the medium of radio offered a host of programming geared to almost every age group. Companies and organizations from most industries would advertise more frequently its product lines. The only industry that predates the radio, in popularity, would be the big screen, with silent movies featuring stars like Rudolph Valentino, Tom Mix, Mae West, Greta Garbo among other stars.

Companies would use this captive audience, so to speak, to advertise their product and merchandise lines.

Most likely the most remembered scenario involving the radio medium took place in the 1950's regarding documentation of the War of the Worlds. Movie great and personality announced during a science-fiction program on the radio announced that there an alien war going on that the population thought was indeed factual. After the programming took place, government officials along with the network contented that it was indeed part of a science-fiction programming. As stated above much of the population in all age groups took the Battle of the Worlds as a real event and they all reacted like it was a legitimate news worthy event. Some individuals, who had the liberty of having insight and inside knowledge of this occurrence claim that the entire announcement was not really a total falsehood. The United States government may have proof to this occurrence and some representatives seem to support this contention. Whether these events did or did not occur is not under debate and nor will there be evidence documented to support either contention. The truth that can be confirmed is the hysteria among the population on all levels and the aftermath or results from such hysteria. The evolution of radio grew especially in the 1950's before the development of the medium of television. The angle consisted of the science fiction form of entertainment of the war of the worlds, which was presented by Orson Welles. This concept was so real in its presentation that the population especially in the North American continent believed that it was real. This is not to state that other science fiction formats occurred earlier, but in no way, did it create the hysteria on several levels. The radio concept forever grew from news, music, sporting events and other events taken place throughout the world.

Naturally, the medium of radio grew as the century progressed. It was still used for advertisement by nearly industry, although the format did change with the times. The era of talk radio, what became known as shock jocks (who occupied different times of the day and broadcast regions throughout the country) and lastly the format of the type of music broadcast by different stations. This was dominated by AM stations until the evolution of what is classified as Rock-n-Roll, Country, Pop and other types of music which was started by music production by

Chuck Berry, Little Richard, Billy Haley and the Comets, Elvis Presley (deemed the king of Rock-n-Roll), Buddy Holley, Richie Valens, Johnny Cash, Roy Orberson, The Beatles, The Rolling Stones, The Doors, Led Zeppelin, Michael Jackson (deemed the king of Pop), Kenny Rogers and list seems endless just as the types of music formats changed. These stations specialized in promoting every music taste imaginable from Country, Pop, Rock, Classical, Rap and much more. Some formats stayed the same broadcasting news and sporting events. These broadcast stations, like the new medium of television centered on in this case what the listener's demands were and expanded to 24 hours a day. With the availability of these types of music the FM era was born, along with a new concept called music on the television. Certain stations would broadcast music using different scenarios like concert footage, groups putting together their own footage and other types of productions. This concept enabled different musical groups to keep themselves in the limelight and introduce new types of music to the public in order to gauge whether there was a significant demand for these bands to tour or put out music in first records, then tapes, cassettes, CDs, DVDs, etc. It is important to keep in mind that this concept was not just limited to just music as every form of entertainment seem to be benefitted from this advancement and growth can be illustrated and measured in each industry.

The Entertainment Industry also benefited and advanced through the century, whereas the industry consisted of live performances up to the 20th century. The first electronic recorded mechanism widely available to the population was an item called the record. People from different entertainment fields (comedy, music, poetry, etc.), the educational field and everything in between would create what became known as albums. For a cost, it would be available to the population. As illustrated it started with live performances and within this aspect as technology evolved so did the shows, concerts, etc., insomuch became more sophisticated because of the utilization of discoveries like the lasers and computer animation.

The evolution of radio grew especially in the 1950's before the development of the medium of television. The angle consisted of the science fiction form of entertainment of the war of the worlds, which was presented by Orson Welles. This concept was so real in its presentation that the population especially in the North American continent believed that it was real. This is not to state that other science fiction formats occurred earlier, but in no way, did it create the hysteria on several levels. The radio concept forever grew from news, music, sporting events and other events taken place throughout the world. The concept did not stop in the 1960's as the medium continued to be a launching pad for the industries listed above, but music venues of all types of fields benefited a widespread audience. It would be remiss to not include religion in this venue. It is important to note that AM radio broadcasting was the initially starting point, but as the century progressed to the ladder part; approximately twenty-five years FM radio, which featured shock jock broadcasters, political broadcasters and most of the formats were still in place from the initial beginning.

Chapter 10

Movies with sound

Before any discussion of movies with sound, the relatively short period that was not only in black and white, but also silent must also be examined. Stars like Rudolph Valentino, Mae West, Greta Garbo and Tom Mixx are among the short list of several stars that created an industry that eventually led to what is now referred to the Golden Age of Hollywood or movie making. There seemed to be an abundance of talent to entertain fans of any subject matter in any age group. As mentioned above, it was a short time in respect to the industry but it took live entertainment off the limited stage to the big screen. It did not eliminate live entertainment, as it was used in concert with it to this present day.

This industry in some ways was not really an advancement, but not to include it would really leave the century incomplete because of the contributions of the industry on so many levels. Initially the movies, as stated above, had its own allure to the public. It started in isolated buildings much like live entertainment and the silent movies did before it. Live entertainment such as the theater, shows, plays (which the best known took place in areas like Broadway, New York and in other areas throughout the country), concerts by musical entertainers and other concepts. Movies were really in a category all by itself, whether it was silent, sound and eventually sound with color. The addition of color changed and enhanced the industry, which help to increase the movie going population. This concept was around sometime before the birth of television, which will be covered next. It truly gave the public or population an escape for a couple of hours that took them away from the real issues surrounding everyday life. Practically every form of movie was eventually made from subject matter regarding action, westerns, gangster, romance, detective mysteries, fiction, non-fiction, science-fiction, thrillers, horrors, musicals and everything in between. Eventually, it seemed that nothing was taboo and stars from this industry were created over-night. It was and is a unique form of entertainment.

As stated above the settings for these movies were usually in isolated buildings by other businesses, which again allowed these other businesses to lure the movie going public to their establishment. It would be commonplace when someone would mention a movie, the thought of Hollywood, California immediately comes to mind, just as a show, the thought of Broadway, New York has the audience in the same mindset, but in reality, just like plays, concerts and shows were done throughout the world. Where ever there was an audience large enough to generate revenue and naturally a demand issue was a major component as it is today. The term of being shot or done on location became commonplace as the industry grew and became more popular. Like any other industry and the movie industry is no exception, it created stars within its own (for examples Edward G. Robinson, Humphrey Bogart, Gary Cooper, Henry Ford, Cary Grant, Grace Kelly, Lauren Bacall, Lucille Ball, John Wayne, Clint Eastwood, Marlon Brando, Tommy Lee Jones, Sharon Stone, Sylvester Stallone and so many others; the list seems endless) and there were what can be best termed as crossover stars like Bing Crosby, Frank Sinatra, Mario Lanza, Doris Day, Shirley Jones, Bob Hope, Elvis Presley and that list as above seems endless. There is no intention to leave anyone out of all the lists of stars of this industry, as it would fill a book all by itself in order to truly do it justice. They all made contributions in entertainment already established on television and on the horizon.

The point including this industry as influential in the 20th century is that the allure of the movie first in an isolated building allowed businesses and organizations to advertise their product lines to a captive audience so to speak. Like any other industry in this century both established and new it evolved to meet customer demand and maximize on the potential profit from all productions. Normally, movies would have an advertised start time, but there was always a push by the theater in this case for the audience to be made aware of the snack area, which featured a product line of popcorn, name brand candy and soft drinks. The theater or movie dwelling offered a host of start times ranging from matinees to different movie start times throughout the evening, which often differed on the weekends. As these movie dwellings developed there was a new concept that appealed especially to the younger generation in the era called drive-ins. The movie goer would have the luxury of sitting in his or her vehicle next to a speaker that provided sound, watching a movie on a gigantic screen and the next movie goer being a few feet from them. Naturally, the same advertisement in the regular movie dwelling would still be advertised, but the movie goer would have privacy to a point never conceived or enjoyed in a movie going setting. Of course, the major setback would be weather conditions at the time of the showing. However, over-all drive-ins were major money makers on several levels including the industry itself, the drive-in dwelling and product lines that were advertised before and during the movie itself. Early in the industry's history there was always an effort to conceal the merchandise identity during the before mentioned movie or production. This notion changed as the popularity of movies for every age group increased beyond all expectations. Organizations started to recognize the revenue possibilities throughout the population. Most likely the success in marketing product lines through the relatively new medium of television on several levels opened the doors of advertising in this fashion and the instant and over-all success of several organizations that utilized this mode. Naturally, the movie industry had to be subtle than mentioned in the section of television; for an example, it could not utilize two former baseball legends like Mickey Mantle and Whitey Ford debating whether Miller Lite Beer was less filling or tasted great. This concept gradually changed as organizations found an avenue to present name brand merchandise in the very movie presentation itself. This is not to state that merchandise and product lines were not in a movie presentation, but there was always a concentrated effort not to mention or advertise the manufacturer's name. This started to gradually change towards the end of the century, where product lines were either directly or indirectly advertised in the movie.

The amazing part of the allure of the movie industry within the population was yet to happen as we progressed through the century. It would not be accurate to relate that the movie industry never had the allure to the population as described above, because as live entertainment, the population wanted an escape from reality of the times and era. It is easy today to examine the past century acknowledging all the progress, but conveniently having amnesia to the facts that there were two world wars, several other wars, so-called conflicts, recessions, gas and energy crisis and the Great Depression of the 1930's. Is it any great wonder why the population wanted and needed a temporary escape for a couple of hours? One very interesting fact is that infamous gangster, John Dillinger, was caught outside a movie theater where he was shot and killed. This just shows the allure of the movie industry to the entire population.

No one, but perhaps a few could ever imagine how the movie industry would eventually influence other industries both established and on the horizon. It seemed that each town or city would have an abundance of theaters featuring movies geared and targeted towards each part of the population, which extended different rated movies in the same theater at different parts of the day. Theaters evolved into showing anywhere from a few features to several features in the very same dwelling. This was accomplished by showing movies in large sound proof rooms, where the capacity for seating depended on the size of each room. The rating system G, PG, R, X-XXX. It was based on the adult content of the feature, which would start with approval for children to adult only. This was based on language, violence, nudity, sex, etc. These theaters were strategically located for several reasons, which include to improve the number of people to a geographical location where other types of businesses were operating that improved revenue.

In essence these theaters would serve multi-purposes, first for movie goers to go to the establishment to see the movie and secondly as a draw for customers to shop at other businesses for what can be best described as the impulse buy. At first these theaters would be located in the same general geographical location of other businesses for such a scenario. The presentation of movies would be at different time slots, whereas all types of restaurants and other businesses would benefit from walk-in traffic. This served two purposes, first as described above the impulse buy or to let potential customers know that the organization was in the area for future purchases and business. This would be especially beneficial to restaurants, fast food establishments and other type of retailers operating in virtually every industry.

Another operating scenario were the operation of these movie theaters in both a small and large shopping mall atmosphere or scenario. The format of operation would be literally the same as described above, with some real differences. These theaters would be geographically located in the same shopping mall with both large established businesses and the small independent businesses. Each would benefit from the drawing power that each offered the customer. The theme to always seem to center around advertisement, whether it was a food product or other merchandise advertised directly or indirectly in the movie presentations. The goal always seems to center around trying to get the movie goer interested in the product line being illustrated or introduced in the feature presentation.

The following operating scenario, which was a huge money maker for the movie industry would be the concept of the multiplexes. These would consist of several large movie theaters operating in a single dwelling. The theory was to offer several movies viewing opportunities to the large segment of the movie goer population. Each age group was targeted in this scenario, where the concept was to offer several opportunities and again the idea to draw revenue from the local population that may have different agendas than what was originally intended, but the results as illustrated above were identical to the single theater.

One consistent concept that has been a constant throughout the history of humanity and there had been several, is the appeal and longevity of entertainment. No matter which society is examined, researched or studied this can be found in almost every culture in history. We have witnessed several forms of entertainment ranging from everything conceivable, whether it is sports, musically performances, the recently mentioned movies above, plays and everything in between. This would include cruelty to anything else that can be conceived by humanity. This along with other such events can be used as a measuring stick to show once again how much we have not changed no matter how civilized

The 20th Century...The Real Truth

we think that we have become, yet we have not really shifted in our philosophy towards others.

The allure of the medium of television allowed organizations to advertise their product line to the wider audience, to that point, to a much larger basis never before achieved in any retail audience or environment. The industry never before dreamed of an outreach in such a wider segment of the population format ever achieved in any medium prior to that era. The natural result an increase in profits and brand name recognition never before witnessed in markets not within the normal geographical locations of what the organization would naturally refer to as its market area.

Naturally, to document the movie industry without pay per view, which started towards the end of the 1900's would make this incomplete. Organizations in different industries were already in the midst of advertising within the movie presentation itself. This enabled the movie goer population to watch newly released movies in a relatively short period of time. As mentioned above new movies would have a premiere period of time in the theaters, but with pay per view this period of time grew shorter in reference to the period of time. There would be a cost to view a new movie in this format, but the population can view it conveniently in the privacy of their own home. This did evolve as we progressed into the 21st century and the concept called Netflix and other companies sped up the process to where new movies are often available within a week of the release. Of course, there is a substantial cost for these movies to be available to the population. Part of this concept is to view these movies on the individual's personal computer, which is truly amazing considering the limited time that the industry has evolved and where the industry was a mere 100 years ago.

Most likely the most amazing part or essence of the movie industry is not how it necessarily directly influenced other industries in our society, but how it indirectly influenced our culture and how certain issues were felt by others throughout the world. To witness how live entertainment influenced humanity throughout the centuries cannot be truly measured. What is really amazing is to examine, evaluate and truly study how the industry changed our society on so many levels. The impact on the educational level is a phenomenon that can be measured in the early stages of the industry and again mentioned so many times as this study is being conducted, which would be the future impact on society as the world moves into the future and more importantly what can be learned as we progress into the future on what can be really learned and grow as a society. The real fascination will definitely come from what was truly loss in the documentation as our world and society moves forward in the 21st century and beyond. Losing brilliance, ingenuity and insight from Albert Einstein there are still leagues of mountains and mountains of information that we still must learn as a civilization and society to realize our full potential. As being humanity, this growth potential may never be realized. The proof of this is never more proven than the history of humanity.

Old televisions

Chapter 11

Television

What is really amazing is in comparison of other industries, the television industry became well established in a very short period of time. This really became the definition of entertainment for more than a generation and its full realization has still not been achieved as it still evolves as entertainment for all age groups in the population. The illustration of the first television was big and bulky plus initially only being available to certain segments of the population until companies like RCA and other organizations mass produced them, thus making them more affordable. The part that might be hard to imagine to the younger generation, who were born in the 1980's or later were the facts that there were television antennas to pick-up major network broadcasts, really only three national networks (ABC, CBS and NBC), only a few local or regional networks and perhaps a limited amount of Public Broadcast Stations; all this depended on the strength of the broadcast tower and the type of antenna plus geographical location was also a factor. There were also other realities, for examples the end of the broadcast day between midnight to one AM (no 24- hour a day broadcasting), the showing of the American flag and the playing of the national anthem; afterwards everything would go into a snow-like effect. There was no satellite, cable, VCR, DVD or Blu-ray disc players.

Initially in the birth or inception of the medium of television had a host of influences in its growth process. This medium had a host of intentions that contributed to the beginning, development and agenda that influenced to the advertisement of product and merchandise lines that had immediate results felt from this medium. This took place throughout its history and was short in comparison to other resources, either established, in its infancy or at best can be documented in phases, which would be completed well beyond the idea or planning categories. The popularity varied to everything to include news, sports and entertainment. This very concept developed from live entertainment, to movies, which were initially black and white; but now were in the well-established and familiar present state of color and sound. The idea for this medium was to take the population for anything to beyond in time in order to temporarily escape the real issues and problems taken place locally, nationally and globally. Truthfully the main purpose was to take the audience or population away from reality for whatever time span away consciously of the reality of what events were factually happening in the real world around them.

This idea is and was fine if people or the audience understood that this medium was just an escape for a short period of time and not the real answers facing each part of society's real problems and issues. To equate this medium was just an escape and advertising tool; the fact to equate for reality would be classified as foolish and ignorant. This box that initially had analog electronics, transistors and a small or large viewing picture tube is and was a far solution to what humanity is or were a far illustration of true reality. This scenario illustrated as reality has been taken place since the birth of humanity, but now because of this medium called television has put these barbaric and disgusting acts on the world's stage, if one could be so bold to illustrate this sad reality. Human Beings have been doing these disgusting acts for centuries; it was just magnified because of this medium. This was termed as immediate news until the escalation of the Internet. How does the action or violence of taken innocent lives be justified or forward these actions? This must be the paramount question or query that must be answered if we truly want to advance as a society or culture.

Virtually every industry used this medium to advertise their product line and some classical commercials advertising everything for all age groups were targeted. Some classic commercials would involve fast food like Kentucky fried chicken pushing 'get a bucket of chicken' to McDonald's famous familiar push of 'two all- beef patties, special sauce, lettuce, cheese, pickles, onions and on sesame bun or you deserve a break today.' The famous soft drink push of 'We are the Pepsi generation', 'The Real Thing' from Coke Cola and that famous lite beer from Miller Taste Great and less Filling. These commercials did not include only fast food and drinking products, whereas clothing lines, shoe lines, services, alcohol, cigarettes, stores of all types and everything in between. These are just a few examples and there were advertisement campaigns for almost every industry; both established and new. In reality these organizations dedicated their advertising budget to gain beyond just a local or region market. There were concentrated efforts to gain market shares nationally and globally.

It would be a falsehood or incorrect to illustrate that the medium of television is just portrayed as a negative impact on our over-all society or culture. This would be illustrating just half the facts about television. There are and were honorable programming and networks that both brought non-bias news and educate its audience. Eventually, there were entertainment venues that attracted audience within the population to forms of programming established years and decades earlier by the movie industry. The programming by the television industry emulated the programming well established by the movie industry, which utilized a formula that was very successful. They targeted the population by age, sex, geographical location, content of the programming and other factors. The reality is by the 1950's to the 1960's it was commonplace to have a television in most households and it was the source of news, education, sporting events and other entertainment well established or just beginning in that era. The new concept of the television series was just in its infancy.

The fact as illustrated above is that the television industry is somewhat younger in comparison to most other industries. It is commonplace to forget that the evolution and growth of the industry took place very quickly. The first television consisted of transistors, picture tubes, other tubes, primitive analog electronics and other components. The unit was very heavy and there was also a limit as far as screen size. Within the next so-called generation of the television, the advancements in technology concerning sound quality, an increase in screen size, improvements in utilizing color, the evolution of analog electronics and other components produced a very different type of television. As the century ended the concept of digital electronics actually revolutionized the television closer to a product available to the population in today's market. The television that once weighed well over 100 pounds, with a much smaller viewing screen has changed a great deal. Although, initially the television produced at the end of the century were much lighter in weight, a larger viewing screen, improvement in the quality in sound and other components that improved the television; the initial availability was an issue and problem for the population. The first major hurdle was cost of the unit, although the quality of the unit was leagues above the initial unit, with a superior sound system, what was termed as theater size viewing screens (that seem to get larger every year), along with the unit being much lighter and other improvements. The list seems endless as each year of the evolution process does produce an improved product. The quality of the viewing screen kept improving as the 9-mil meter became outdated with projectors composed with then new electronics called analog. It was a concept with both electronics initially at first. Although the analog electronics was bulky than the next evolution called digital electronics, it was more reliable than the older 9 mil meter projector and allowed for more advancements like sound and eventually color. As illustrated in the television, along with the combination of tubes, transistors and analog electronics it helped the develop of the television take place in the 1950's. When the century progressed the invention or evolution of the digital electronics affected every form of electronic established to that point in history and in many ways provided new forms of electronics that were only in the dreaming state or on the blackboard, so to speak.

The new concept of theater type sound illustrated as first stereo sound took hold that improved the sound of movies and programming on television was revolutionary as the concept of technicolor in movies and eventually television. The concept of sound within whole industry including music, radio, television and movies were on an evolution course in which would improve the quality beyond expectations. This new concept did not stop there as it seems that all forms of entertainment was involved in this evolution concept. Live concerts with the popular artists of the era were moving beyond just the sound effects, where they would utilize the evolution of visual effects. This would involve more than a musical artist or band performing on stage. The use of visual special effects would involve several that would include laser light shows along with other methods to both involve and entertain the audience.

As described above the evolution of the television grew a great deal in the ladder part of the century. This growth was due to the advancements in the electronic field, especially with analog and digital electronics. Initially, at the start of what is referred to as the television era; the 25-inch screen was considered large and very heavy. The weight of the unit was because of its composition. Towards the end of the century and beginning of the 21st century, the 25-inch television is considered small in comparison to the larger screen. This was due to the advancements in digital electronics that help create what is referred to 'theater screens'. These units were much lighter as picture tubes and other tubes became obsolete.

Cable wires

First Flat Screen Television

Chapter 12

Cable and Satellite

The development of this advancement really was the follow-up to more than one industry. Although, it was not really an advertisement follow-up to both the radio and television, it was still developed to advertise to consumers in their very own homes. Indirectly, however, in the initial stages it brought consumers out of their homes to theaters that were starting to open in major shopping malls where retailers could use the concept of these theaters as more as a to draw to the shopping malls. This ended to a point due to the birth of cable and satellite, because as this entertainment venue entered our society, the population discovered a new avenue to view movies, sporting events and other forms of entertainment. This created a new concept of commercial free television, which is somewhat new except for television with some limited commercials, which sponsored the program being aired. As illustrated this normally took place after midnight in the early morning hours, with some exceptions.

The cable industry came first in the late 1970's and early 1980's. At first it featured movies that already been seen in theaters and normally there was a span of time for movies to what can be best described as an exclusive time format for theaters outside the population's individual homes. The programming would follow somewhat closely what the television industry had done initially, whereas the target were all age groups in the population. There was an effort to offer programming geared for the younger age group in the day or early evening and the adults were targeted in the evening hours. The cable companies would air popular movies from the past, until the newer movies had its runs in theaters in planning time periods as stated above. Not all cable companies necessarily followed the age group theme, but they did as far as the newer movies were concerned. It is important to keep in mind that cable companies were not as wide spread as they are today. Initially, there was a limit of providers to offer the population access to the programming that cable offered. There was also an evolution process in terms of areas of availability and growth of companies or organizations throughout most of the world.

The main channels initially were Home Box Office and Showtime, which initially aired movies throughout the day. Both channels evolved to feature different types of entertainment that included boxing, concerts involving all kinds of music, specials with different comedians and other programming targeting all age groups. The cable industry was not limited to the format described above, whereas it expanded to different channels that featured different programming popular with the population in a specific geographical region or location. The industry developed packages of entertainment that was made available on every level imaginable; ranging from income level, sex, geographical location, age and every criterion within the population. This concept and format was not entirely new because it was started by the television industry years earlier, but the fact and results achieved by the cable industry enhanced and grew this concept well beyond all expectations.

The cable industry also grew in size and programming that it could offer to their customers and viewers much like the television industry accomplished in a couple of decades before cable was established. It, however, is not the best industry for such a comparison, because both were very unique in what each industry offered to the consumer base in their population region. The expansion of cable in the industry was another great example of the theme of the 20th century.

Initially, cable industry featured movies and very little of anything else, but that all changed as the industry added series type programming that basically included every theme available on television. It added special boxing events that really expanded the industry to new heights in entertainment. Yet it did not stop with just special sporting events and programming like boxing, as it grew into other entertainment areas like the National Football League and other programs that appealed to its audience in nearly age group. It was initially somewhat limited, where movie channels were Home Box Office (HBO) and Showtime (SHO). In addition, it would feature different music channels like MTV and others, where musical singers or groups would shoot video with the song or they may have some concert footage of the performances from the past. Naturally, like any other industry in the century it was constantly evolving and the choice of channels expanded to meet the population's wants as far as stay at home entertainment. This evolution included keeping the popular television broadcast stations as well as some addition on new channels. The concept of limited channels, which was ushered in with the birth of television ended as cable became more affordable and wanted by the population as the century entered its last 20 or so years. This is not a claim that the television industry ended by any means, but it was enhanced with more broadcast stations than any time in its illustrious history. In reality the two industries combined, whereas the long-established broadcast stations along with new stations combined with the evolving cable industry. To this point it did set a new standard as far as variety and quality of entertainment. There was no longer an end to the broadcast day, where television broadcast stations would stop programming at a certain hour; instead along with new stations would continue broadcasting 24 hours a day. With the addition of other broadcast stations, the population had variations and a choice of themes of entertainment that they wished to view. The viewing options widen even further with championship and other boxing matches with top names competing in the era, the before mentioned paid per view events and movies and other broadcasts that were popular with the viewing population (programming included new programs about the NFL, MLB and other programs that targeted certain parts popular with the viewing population).

The true evolution was yet to come as the cable industry expanded its services beyond just as a movie, musical and sports venue for the population. As mentioned prior the paid per view venue expanded to meet the viewing population's wants and demands. The movie and other entertainment venues were just the beginning, whereas the expansion of services included telephone services and a brand-new concept as the internet super highway that touched nearly every industry both established and new.

Satellite was really an expansion of the cable industry; whereas the viewing options really expanded far more than the cable industry could offer the population. In essence it was a step up beyond cable. The full benefits of satellite have not been fully realized, where it would be almost comparing the differences of cable and television broadcast stations, where it was really nothing as far as quality of the television industry to the cable industry. The evolution of the satellite industry is still relatively young and its full impact has not been fully realized as an entertainment venue for the population. The satellite industry was really in its infancy at the end of the 20th century. Like the rest of the industries, especially towards the ladder part, the cost of having a satellite system was quite expensive and only the elite could afford it. That changed as the industry grew in the first part of the 21st century offering more than what the cable industry offered.

older Satellite and the receiver

Chapter 13

The Computer and Internet

The birth of computer technology took place in the late 1930's where Bell Laboratories was founded in 1937 and Hewlett-Packard was founded in 1939. There were other discoveries for basically military reasons in Germany, England and the United States during World War II. Initially most of first inventors were mathematicians, other inventors evolved the technology for different industries. It is important to note that other industries grew and were refined because of the evolution of computer technology.

As early as 1946, the University of Pennsylvania's Moore School of Electrical Engineering offered courses in computer technology. These were taught by early computer pioneers along with mathematicians. Classes like these not only influenced further development in the industry, but influenced other universities and colleges throughout the world to offer similar classes. The list of early computer pioneers and mathematicians seem to be endless and fill a four-year degreed college program illustrating the brilliant minds involved. It would make a great subject matter for several books. These schools produced more pioneers that helped the computer field to constantly evolve, which is still taken place well into the 21st century (today). Just to highlight some of the lecturers included were original computer pioneers such as John von Neumann, John Mauchly and J. Presper Eckert, along with mathematicians George Stibilz, Douglas Harter and Derrick Lehmer. Their students were equally impressive, which consisted the likes as Maurice Wilkes, David Rees, Jay Forrester and Claude Shannon. This format inspired the next generation, which included BINAC, EDSAC and eventually the IAS machine the next copies of the AVIDAC. As in every field there are more brilliant minds like Steve Wozniak, who developed the personal laptop computer that closely resembles the computers that are available today.

The birth of the computer was publicly made known shortly after World War ll and it was nothing close to the image that comes to mind today in describing the modern computer. Like any other invention or discovery there was an evolution period and these first computers, which became available in the 1970's hardly came close to personal computers available towards the end of the century. These computers could not be used for entertainment purposes to play games, personal programming and numerous other tasks. Naturally, for a price there were some exceptions. The original computers available in the 1970's was big, bulky and came in some cases smaller computers were geared more towards a customer for hobby reasons. Another enormous difference was there was not any programming in comparison what is common today with the much smaller personal computer. One of the first successful functioning was called the Electronic Numerical Integrator Analyzer and Computer (ENIAC), which was constructed at the University of Pennsylvania in the United States. Its main function was for use by the United States military during World War ll. The cost for constructing this massive computer was around half million dollars. The computer's make-up consisted of several individual lights, cables, vacuum tubes and an enormous number of switches. The vacuum tubes were essential because it would connect each part of the computer to the other parts. The enormous unit weighed well over 25 tons, which would require a large room that had ample space for the unit itself and the personnel to operate it.

There was a gap in time between the ENIAC computer and the desktop computers manufactured in the 1970's- 1980's. However, there were several companies that offered different computers, which featured their own software. These included IBM, Atari, Intel, RCA and other organizations throughout the world. Included in these were schools for higher education like MIT, University of Manchester, the above-mentioned University of Pennsylvania and other learning establishments.

Unless there was an interest by an individual in the field, the cost of the operating system was expensive for this era. Computer technology was limited to organizations like airlines (IE SABRE in 1964, which was an IBM and American Airlines computer used for reservations or bookings). Prior to this it was used for space missions specifically for the United States and the Soviet Union in the 1950's to the present time. The company known as Apple developed smaller computers used for the government, military and businesses. They were still very large and expensive, plus the language was very complex. They can only be operated by people with specialized education or training.

Software and the Internet

How can anyone give an honest accounting or history of the 20th century without illustrating the genius and contributions from Mr. Bill Gates, Mr. Allen and the people from Silicon Valley? The Internet, which is part of the computer industry played a key role in the advancements that took place especially in the last part of the century and the beginning of the 21st century. The concept that might be forgotten is first computer industry, which was really both utilized by the government and the military. The idea, initially, behind the use of the computer was to simplify the workings of the government and business organizations on every level and help govern an ever-growing population on every level.

The advancement and development of both the analog and eventually digital electronics played a key role in the growth of the computer industry. As stated above computers were huge and required its own space to be operational. Often there was a main terminal for the computer operator or programmer, but it would be common for an additional office that contained terminals connected to the computer for people to input information. The computer even had had a different language in order to operate or input information. These people were classified as data entry personnel and the size would be reflective and depend on how large the organization and type of operation. The variety as described above ranged on every scale imaginable, which includes businesses on the local, state, national, global and utilized by most governments along with the military.

Communication and utilizing the computer evolved over a period of time from the initial first two apple computers, which took place over a very short period of time in comparison to the other advancements that took place as the computer agency evolved the last part of the century. The major obstacles facing this evolution was the size of the computer and how the population was going to use the computer without complex methods and languages to operate the computer highlighted above. The first step involved a mixture of analog and digital electronics, thus making the computer much smaller that made the computers more affordable to most of the population.

The first personal computer that can be termed was the desk top computer, which was completely different from the first computers developed by Apple and far different what is available in the market through its evolution or growth as far as the follow-up in the immediate years following and what is finally available today in the 21st century. This was the initial step or generation of the personal computer. Naturally the cost of this computer was quite expensive, but the major issue was the cost of operating the computer. The major issue is how to make these computers and programs more user friendly. The organization from Silicon Valley in California has made this more than a reality to most of the population throughout the world. The program expanded with different features to address the needs and wants of their consumers. This in itself was a constant evolution as the computer became more sophisticated and complicated as digital electronics was the major component with a mix of analog electronics. The physical cosmetics of the computer did not change to significantly until upgrades were made to improve the desktop. The computer language of DOS was essential in the beginning and as stated above to have specialists operate and maintain computers was slowly evolving to a more sophisticated system in the use of computers.

The real change came from the geniuses from Silicon Valley, California, where they developed computer language that made it possible for households to have these smaller desktop computers in their individual homes. The famous catch phrase of 'You've Got Mail' became a normal occurrence as people turned on their desktop computers. The evolution of personal computers was just at the starting stage.

Little did the normal population realize that the desktop computer was just the beginning in virtually every industry. This involved working professionals like doctors to college students, which would forever change the world. Even younger children would be touched by this advancement. The evolution of this industry would reach levels involving education, research, entertainment and seem to have no limits to the extent that no one could ultimately imagine at its inception. Witnessing the growth since the computer's inception to just the end of the 20th century, one must admit pure amazement. The evolution of the industry in the first part of the 21st century would include laptops, tablets, notebooks, I-pads and sophisticated phones that have Internet capability. This just names a few items that technology has produced during such a limited time in the industry's history.

The computer industry definitely achieved heights by all expectation on every level conceivable in every industry that utilized this advancement. Most experts feel that it still has not achieved its full potential and its full evolution is still not realized as our society grows into the 21st century. The most amazing fact about computer science is that the truth about this technology like the comparison of other technologies started in the 20th century is the fact that the technology or phenomenon is still very young and can grow exponentially. To state that the discovery of the computer and the direct result from it referred to as the Internet was one of the most significant discoveries of the 20th century would be an understatement to say the least. There were several advancements throughout the history of humanity, but not to state that the discovery of the computer would leave a tremendous gap in relating the advancements in the 20th century. Computer Science has played such an important role in so many advancements throughout the century.

The Internet as alluded to above was used by nearly every organization to the population that had access to this marvel. At first it would use the already established telephone lines to enable the customer or population to gain access. If one truly examines and evaluates the Internet, it was like having a Sunday paper (which was full of advertisements for every industry or service available to the population) virtually 24 hours a day/ seven day a week. As it evolved it became more than just a tool for news, communication, social events, education and advertisement for organizations; with a host of agendas and goals they wanted to achieve. It was more than the statement stated above than 'You've Got Mail.'

The population can virtually do research on any product or manufacturer that they are considering doing business with, whether the subject matter is an automobile, a toy for a child and everything in between. One does not have to view to far back in history to view experts' and consumers' reports regarding almost every product or item available on the market. It started to expand the boundaries of the definition of research on every level, which eventually extended to professionals and students. It eventually became the ultimate library with the world of knowledge as close to the keyboard and monitor within the operator's fingertips. The birth of the information age as we perceive it was on the verge of becoming a reality of being born and becoming establishing itself as a reality.

Although college libraries, other libraries and bookstores were still part of the landscape at universities, colleges and other public areas like different types of mall settings, the Internet or the information super highway (as it started to be referred to) started to replace the old modes listed above. The mode of research started to shift that included everything from high school to doctorate thesis, which started to note more web site addresses than books and encyclopedias. Professionals and students on all levels used website addresses to access professional quotes or educated points of view to support theories noted in papers and thesis. Each region of universities and colleges publish books on how each reference would be noted in the reference page, which the supporting expert quote or fact would be normally inserted within the said written work and the complete information would be illustrated on the reference page. There would be books on how each higher educational resource that how each reference was listed and outlined. Each region or learning facility seemed to have its own preference on how each was formatted.

The only reason to mention these changes in something minuscule as an educational paper, project or thesis is to high light the changes by the Internet in something that might seem minor or insignificant. However, examining changes as small or minor as a reference for an educational paper should and can give one a hint of the larger significant changes for the future in the governmental and corporate setting. As the old adage states the devil is in the details, which will be something and the real main fact for generations and decades to come. Teaching that concept early to upcoming generations can help eliminate so many mistakes.

It is difficult to end the significant changes by the computer and the Internet in our society, thus stopping at 2000 would be impossible. The reason is that it would seem incomplete without mentioning a young and brilliant programmer who started a website for people to exchange pictures. His name is Mr. Mark Zuckerberg and he was already recognized by the industry as a genius, insomuch that he turned down 1 million dollars for one of several of his game programs that he invented. The offer was made by Microsoft and the website he started was Facebook, which became a social media phenomenon in the early part of the 21st century. His dream was huge and his vision had an immense impact of not only what the Internet is today, but also the entire industry including gaming programs. He is a genius and brilliant because as stated above he created a simple web site to exchange pictures and turned it into a social media site filled with all the intangibles that gives the population great joy and happiness.

The Computer

Chapter 14

The Retail Process and Retail

Originally there were four or more steps within the retail process. The manufacturer/inventor would first create the product or prototype, which so many of my professors referred to as 'widgets.' The term widget is or was defined for our purpose as any product created and manufactured for retail sales and consumer use. This can include infant products to merchandise developed for the elderly and everything or anything in between that has any worth to the general public and creates revenue for the organization. Again, it is essential to stress that the product would be defined as anything that represented value to the individual or customer. As the market became different and obsolete needs for a more elaborate system changed due to consumer sophistication, thus the system became different due to technology and other upgrades in the retail process.

Initially, there were several steps in the retail process or sector. The first step was in the hands of the inventor, then the second step were in the hands of the manufacturers, followed by the wholesalers, who often played the role of the distributors, the next role would be the transportation system to get the merchandise into the hands of the retailer and the next to final step were to the customer. This process would be in constant evolution as the mode of technology and transportation would be constantly changing. The country and the world would be made smaller with the growth rate of the automobile and trucking industry.

The retail industry is and were forever revolving; it could be best described as a work in progress. The fact and true history reflects and depicts the first retail stores as mostly mom and pop establishments in towns selling merchandise with a host of products that were essential or needed within a relatively small marketing area or region. The development and advancement of these stores heavily depended on the region or market it was located in. As history shows even in the United States had development or advancements in the industry depending on geographical locations it was located in. Unlike the industry that eventually developed as the country matured, because as history shows the original colonies developed at a different pace because of geographical locations. These colonies eventually evolved into states; naturally due to the population expansion and the origination of the country eventually resulted; the United States of America. This country did not start at 50 plus states and territories, like any other country it took time to grow to its present status as a country.

Eventually, the theme behind the retail industry grew and perhaps in the separation of merchandise specialized depending on not only addressing needed product and merchandise lines addressing geographical areas or a specific market and region. These areas throughout the country were very widespread, in which the only way retailers to get much needed products and supplies were initially through the use of trains in secluded areas and the use of wagon trains driven by horseback. It slowly recognized the emergence of separating merchandise and products by several categories, thus departmentalizing and specializing its soft and hard lines. The idea and fact was a very slow moving process particularly in the United States because of the vastness of the country and the limits, plus there were problems and issues, which were due to the lack of transportation and technology.

The European countries were somewhat ahead initially of the United States since manufacturing organizations were both geographically closer and already well established. This with the fact that the only way for early retailers to sell or market their products and merchandise was by importing and exporting, which could only be done by shipping until other methods through technology made other methods possible. Therefore, retail stores and/or merchandise stores were relatively slow and time consuming at its inception. The terms of a retail organization establishing multiple units and as time elapsed the concept of retail chains to the likes of Sears Roebuck, which eventually led to be known as Sears, Macy's, Gimbals and other larger retail chains eventually filled the department store landscape. These organizations and stores did not only fill the retail landscape, but they took the place in filling both needs and wants of their consumers and the population. This would encompass the essentials for the geographical market. The introduction of new lines of products and merchandise grew the population beyond what the already growing population to just beyond wants and for the first time entered the real concept of advertisement.

Initially the mom and pop retailer gradually dwindled because of the expansion of the population throughout the United States. New larger retailers started to open stores where the market would dictate the demand. This normally first took place in cities throughout the United States then globally because of the increase in the population. Thus, the larger department store retail organization was born. Parts of major cities may have some of these larger retailers, with several independent smaller retailers and specialty shops in between. This shopping experience would extend for city blocks in some major cities. In some of these cities there would be sections integrated with the population involved, in another word still to this day there are signs and reminders from the past, like Little Italy, Little China, etc. There are still retailers, restaurants, etc. that operate in these areas.

As time went on and the theme behind the retail industry and perhaps in the separation of merchandising lines dependent on not only addressing needed product and merchandise lines addressing geographical area of markets. It slowly recognizing the emergence of separating products and merchandise by sex, age, types of product lines and other categories. Perhaps as stated above the time for the merchandise theme were slowly starting to recognize itself in a smaller market than once thought at its emergence. There were the establishment of smaller type shopping malls that consisted of one or two major retailers, with several smaller retailers offering a host and variety of products and merchandise lines. The smaller type malls with smaller independent retailers can in no way compete or survive in a super mall like Woodbridge Center Mall in New Jersey and other malls being built throughout the country and eventually the world, the International Mall, the Citrus Park Mall in Tampa, Florida, the other Malls in Orlando, Florida and the other shopping malls opening all over the world, without the presence of several larger retailers as a draw for consumers.

Perhaps for the first-time national retailers developed product lines that were not in customers' support or demand. They earned such support and created the demand. They started the name-brand era, whereas each retailer started their own name brand. This was the first time that this was truly attempted on a national or global scale. Some of these famous brand names were established in the past like the Winchester Rifle. There were, however, new brand names like Rawlings, Spaulding, the RCA appliance line, some famous clothing lines, the Coleman manufacturing in camping, the Garcia manufacturing in fishing, the Sears tool line and other product lines that came later. They were other brand names, globally, that were scattered throughout the era. These lines were not limited as nearly every facet had a specialized line known, which included everything from clothing to sporting goods to everything that can be marketed in between.

The beginning of Discount Retail has really developed several ways at different times throughout Department Retail history and technically developing through different ways. It seemed that each retailer had humble beginnings in each part of the United States, which most experts agree that it took place after World War ll and the 1950's. The most recognizable name from the era is Walmart, which was started by Sam Walton. He started out with as a retailer, who operated 5-dime stores in the middle upper part of the United States. Unfortunately, one of his stores had a fire, which was fortunate for him in a way because it forced him to sell slightly damaged merchandise at a reduced price. This spawned an idea to where he would buy merchandise in bulk and price the products or merchandise below what the larger department store chains would normally charge. This would make normally not affordable merchandise accessibly to the poor and emerging middle class. Sam Walton (Walmart) is definitely the standout in this concept because he literally built a multi-billion-dollar organization before his death and the organization is now establishing market shares literally worldwide. The company grew in bulk retail membership and the advantage through the new Internet technology, which will be explained and expanded later in this publication.

As stated above Discount Retail has really developed by several unique and imaginative ways depending on which organization are being researched, studies and examined. The general technique or philosophy behind each of these organizations were to buy these lines of merchandise by bulk from whichever part of the retail process and sell the merchandise to the consumer at a lower price than other larger and established retailers in the market or region. This was one of many ways that the discount retailer would operate. Another way would be to buy on consignment or better yet was to sublet areas within the store to both soft and hard lines representatives; gaining a share of the profit.

Where Sam Walton was brilliant another what can be termed as an accident took place in the New Jersey market; outside the old RCA building, whereas a perfect opportunity happened in the time frame after World War ll. A chance tour by a RCA executive to a guy named Hubschman (he was one of two brothers that sold sandwiches next store to the building to employees) where they came across an area of slightly dented, scratched and other imperfections in appliances; among a complete tour of the merchandise being produced, which would include appliances to televisions. A deal was worked out to get the slightly damaged merchandise on consignment for well under cost and sold the said merchandise for well under normal retail price in a matter of days. All they did was print up fliers advertising the merchandise; this accomplished two avenues of success. First very little start-up cost and letting the customers in their immediate community area know about the availability and reasonable cost of the merchandise. As stated above they sold the merchandise for under normal retail price, thus sparking an idea between the two brothers to build a chain of stores in the New Jersey, New York, Pennsylvania and eventually in the California markets. These stores were eventually called Two Guys, which featured an all in one shopping destination. This included everything from a full line grocery store, which included, a complete soft and hard lines departments. The discount department store chain started in the late1940's and the 1950's through the early 1980's and for unknown reasons the company decided that real estate offered a better revenue source than the retail industry for over-all profit. Thus, the retailer went out of the retail business in the early 1980's. Although well- known names started in the 1950's that promoted and started highly successful organizations, for an example Home Depo, could have posed profits well beyond what could be expected by normal retail outlets or chains. Two Guys were not the only discount retailer that grew in the New Jersey, New York and Pennsylvania, which is considered in the tristate area. There were other organizations like Korvettes, Bambergers, Kmart, Sears, Woolworths, Walmart, Caldors and other discount organizations grew and did well in developing shares in a highly competitive market and region.

The fact that other retailers did very well in the region in question as well as other regions throughout the country. As earlier mentioned in the development of the shopping mall scenario, that it also appeared to a certain market share in the region as well as other parts of the country. The appeal of specializing and name brand merchandise seemed to always be present in what can be best termed as the retailing revolving and ongoing revolving door of opportunity. The question that never really has an answer is does anything really go out of style? It seems like it disappeared from the limelight for a few years or a period of time, but it always seems to return. What but really seems to be almost comical is that when comes back most customers think that it is better than the merchandise ever first developed or they treat it completely new or have complete amnesia about the merchandise when it first established in the market and they have complete amnesia about the merchandise about the impact to the market or region.

The industry did grow in every direction that technology would provide, first there was the marketing through the medium of television; called info commercials. These would be normally half hour time spots sponsored by manufacturers to sell their product lines. These would take place normally after regular programming after midnight, early in the morning hours. The real marvel was yet to come, which was the birth of the Internet. The concept was the answer to the industry's prayers, on how to reach the consumer 24 hours a day; seven days a week. This concept was really an aftermath since the development of the medium of television. Commercials, initially called sponsors, would use this medium to make their merchandise and product lines known to a wider audience of consumers than any other medium up to that point in history. What is truly amazing is the medium of television was really developed within seventy years ago. The illustration of the Internet, which is examined more thoroughly in the technology opened avenues of advertisement to consumers on a worldwide basis and illustrated above plus within the technological chapter just continually grows and the full impact is yet to be fully realized even now within the first quarter of the 21st century. It is now commonplace for established organizations as well as new organizations to meet their consumers' needs and wants on a more consistent basis and until the technology that produced new venues through the Internet these were never fully realized.

As for the medium of television it did not stop as stated above. The audience demanded a wider variety of programming and the concept of ending the broadcast day just seem to disappear as more networks started to emerge offering more choices to the audience in not only every age group locally, regionally and nationally, which took place towards the end of the century. Needless to illustrate that organizations that conducted advertisements through this medium were excited at the possibility of reaching a wider audience in this transition.

The use of technology, specifically, the Internet opened more than an advertising avenue for almost all the components in the previously illustrated retail process and allowed expansion of other retail avenues. This allowed manufacturers to present its product lines in a format never seen before in history. These organizations, who can be located halfway across the state, country and even the world to expand both their product line exposure and literally have no geographical limitation. It would be a falsehood to state that this opportunity was first provided by the Internet, because organizations, other businesses and manufacturers were also reaching their consumers through the mediums of radio and television, but with somewhat limited success. As stated above the Internet gave the population unlimited access to advertisement, product line research and as the Internet matured it gave consumers direct access to the manufacturer's website. This really benefited both the seller and the buyer, which totally enhanced the shopping experience by offering 24-hour a day shopping access.

As highlighted above the entire industry is currently going through an evolution process never witnessed before the in the industry or business world. The format is in a complete reversal and revolution on how business is conducted and this is mainly due to the operation that has changed since the changes to technological shifts taking place on a global scale, which has never before been witnessed in all facets of the business operations never seen in the market plan of strategy to increase market shares basically the result of expansion in over-all presentation only promotes the obvious question; what will be the price this time, at what price for this action would be the result and will the ever nagging of cost be worth the result? How much will be too much? When will be the time when the majority will be heard?

the Satellite

Chapter 15

The Future

This is normally the last chapter of any book, but in this case, it would be appropriate to place it here. As we examine the past and be optimistic about the future, it is easy to forget about past mistakes that humanity has made throughout its history. One can never forget the old adage outlined so many times throughout this publication and our own history has proven that history does indeed repeat itself. It would be so easy to concentrate about the positive advancements in the 20th century, but it would do an injustice to all those who sacrificed sometimes the ultimate price; their own lives. We as a civilization witnessed the good and the bad. The century had several advancements that produced great and significant events, but the opposite also took place and must be acknowledged. The facts that there were the assassination of John F. Kennedy and others, several wars, hunger, epidemics, pan epidemics, terrorism and other events took place in this historically significant century. As stated on the onset of this review or history of the 20th century and there was an honest try to accomplish that goal. But as one looks and more than that studied the past century, it is extremely hard to be objective. The illustration of positive events as anything in human history the negative, corruption, the loss of human life is extreme! It is hard to ignore! How many possible Einsteins have we lost in the name of progress and cruelty, only God can answer that question. Eventually, if we are honest only a careful examination will tell us, but we may not truly ever know; that is probably the truth. As a novice at best in history, the research done as shown that any loss of life, even if it is one, is totally unacceptable to anyone claiming to be civilized and to love God.

Everything is there for the taking and if we are very careful and make the right, moral and ethical decisions; this could be a wonderful world. Sometimes making the right decision takes integrity and courage. Our history is highlighted by such individuals that have displayed those qualities, but unfortunately the same can be said of the opposite. It valuable lessons that can be learned in the process. The point is that there has been a shift in the human thought process to what be best phrased as the 'me thinking' and forgetting that there are literally billions of other human beings on this planet. Things seem to get lost as we live this existence called life. If we as human beings can get past the three main reasons for disagreements, conflicts and wars, which are still religion, economics and real estate; we can have what is termed as a bright future. We have conveniently and purposely forgotten God and the fact that we are just tenants on this third planet in this solar system. Our time is very limited here and getting lost in the 'me thinking' concept has made an extreme change in our culture and philosophy, along with a very important forgotten idea taught to us in our distant past. That is to love each other and more importantly to love Whoever we refer to as our Supreme Being or God. Thoughts about that concept will be shared in the next chapter.

Witnessing the violence around the globe and seeing the needless taking of human life can give one to worry about our future, unless we wake up and do more as a society to stop all this carnage. To wake up and just smell the coffee as the old saying states is not enough anymore. We must elect and push leaders that have integrity if we want any future or real change at all. Our time with the present generation in power is running very short, but it is a very critical time for us as a race and society. Proof of this reality are the mass murders of innocent men, women and children by isolated dictators or leaders in countries throughout the world. These Hitler like philosophies and actions can best be described as criminal and barbaric. The question must be asked, has humanity became civilized in the last century in comparison to nearly 20 centuries earlier when most of the world's population believes that we at best killed the Son of God; or at the very least a Great Prophet? Further documented in this man's ministry that every miracle and deed was to be written down; the world would not have enough books to document all His actions and miracles in His short three-year ministry or history.

If this proves anything; it documents more than just an accidental fad, but truly God's will. The population of well over 1.2 billion Catholics nearly 20 centuries later and not to consider the millions of Christian religions and sects are well beyond a fasting fad that offered no long growth or longevity.

As we approach the first twenty- year mark in the 21st century, we can highlight several positive advancements, but observing what is taking place around the world and in our very own backyards we are handing over a mess. The time for words is over and it must come to action, better yet positive actions. The time for finger pointing about who is at fault has been long time over and if we expect to grow and advance further, everyone must act and most importantly take responsibility. Not to seem over dramatizing the situation, but to put it in sports terms, its 4th down on the 1- yard line in football analogy or it's the bottom of the ninth with the bases loaded and there are two outs, and we need a game ending home-run to win the game.

The 21st century has produced several opportunities for our society to not only grow, but to also do something very special in the realm of history. Imagine leaving our world to upcoming generations something that they can really build upon. It would be refreshing to leave the following generations other notions than here is the world and it is your turn to fix the problems and issues that we left you. We know that was the legacy that we were left with from the last generation. One question among several is that the legacy we want to leave for our future; the next generation and the ones to follow? The comical part about this whole scenario, meaning this book, anyone who proposed a radical idea like my proposal ends up getting threatened or murdered for even suggesting changing the world or our society for the positive. I can tell you from my own personal feelings that I could care less. All I know is that this is the truth and the facts being revealed are nothing but the pure truth, as sad as that reality, which has been stated so many times regarding so many subject matters. As life has taught to so many individuals, some people are not able to handle the truth, but so many history books have been one-sided or flat out lied; one is hard pressed the find the real truth through all the rhetoric. Or to quote one of my favorite saying, which is that the truth will set you free and it is somewhere out there. Can we handle the truth?

It almost seems like people either do not to know or want to hear the real truth no matter how painful or what being real the end results may achieve. Sometimes people are afraid of the truth and looking for others to deal with problems and issues. The real reminder that we all must face is that we need to know which direction we are facing, before we move forward as a society. It is time to take the blinders off and take the cotton out of our ears.

If one would honestly examine the 20th century was the real establishment of the middle class. It was a byproduct of the Industrial Revolution. As the world proceeds through the first part of the 21st century, it is obvious that the middle class is starting to erode away and the world will return to only two classes. This would be classified as rich and poor. Not being an expert in the field, but if one examined the world's economy the unemployment rate really affects two parts of the population. It is conclusive that essentially only segments of the middle and poor classes are most affected. Take for an example the country of the United States, the unemployment rate is only measured by the population receiving compensation. Others that are not eligible are not considered in the statistic. Politicians are elected based on campaign promises made specifically to these segments, but the promises fail to become a reality. If left unchecked and if our politicians keep failing to keep their promises, the middle will erode and be a distant memory as we progress further into the 21st century.

Chapter 16

Final Thoughts

As outlined in earlier chapters and throughout the book, there was a concentrated effort on the author's part to try to remain objective. Truthfully in some cases it was a failure, but in defense it was honesty. We in the country of the United States are coming into an election year. In putting this together over the last year interviews were conducted with several individuals from the well off, to the middle class (when I can find such candidates) and the poor. The feeling that was consistent across all the classes was about the future. We have narrowed the election or race to two individuals and honestly there is some fear and apprehension. These feelings are just putting it mildly and the voices of the majority are being ignored, to keep this politically correct.

First is the Democrat candidate and it seems her supporters have amnesia to put it mildly. After reading several articles from different publications, they are hinting that electing this candidate would be like President Obama's third term in office. Since the candidate's husband was in office, which he did do some positive actions. However, closing our eyes to NAFTA that he signed sent our jobs overseas instead of keeping them here. With that action and the last eight years combined have literally eroded the middle class. The present Democratic candidate made her feelings very clear about United States citizens' right to bear arms; she opposes that right and we have seen countries in the European Union and other countries try that innovative plan, with negative results and a rising crime rate (particularly of home invasions). The bottom line is only law abiding citizens do the legalities of owning a weapon, whereas the criminals get weapons off the streets. The next is twofold letting illegal immigrants into our country and taking the mention of God out on every level. The Democratic candidate supports almost all the above. Instead of letting the illegal immigrants in, here are some radical ideas; why not feed and help our hungry, help the veterans and our own young to get an education. Who knows helping our own citizens may help change the country around, may have positive results and do some good and positive. So much for our Constitution, our founding fathers and all the people who paid for that ultimate price, their families and us. The number one question people asked me is, besides being first lady, name me three things that she has done correct politically. I pondered for an answer to that question for weeks and months. She was Secretary of State, where she had an opportunity to take and rescue both soldiers and people in harm's way or certain death; all she did was made promises and did nothing. As far as the e-mail fiasco, do we want anyone male or female could make that kind of mistake; it is just the magnitude of the incident that is bothersome, because of the errors (they do sell Microsoft, etc. for dummies). All the FBI Director did, was dance around the issue, but if it were you or I; we would be indicted and put in jail. Oh, she did negotiate with Putin from Russia for nuclear arms reduction, which all the evidence shows that we only honored the accord. Even with just four years with that kind of leadership, the Constitution would be destroyed and unrecognizable. Do not get me wrong there is nothing incorrect in electing a woman president, but let set the standards and requirements remain the same for any candidate; LET'S MAKE SURE SHE/HE IS QUALIFIED!?!?! I along with others are not sure that we want someone of that mental magnitude and integrity in the oval office!?! I am not the most computer literate person in the world, in fact I Thank God that there is an on button and I need to study the manual how to do other functions like shutting the computer down. Apart from the President William Clinton administration and the past eight years I was a life-long Democrat and now I am scared for not only me, but also the future generations present and the generations yet to come.

To give equal billing the Republican candidate has no real political experience, but if he surrounds himself with good people like his candidate for Vice President Pence it does give some relief to the United

States citizens and his critics. All through his campaign he was abrasive and a straight shooter. Love him or hate him, he left no question marks where he stood on the issues and one must at the very least appreciate honesty. From the very beginning he made no secret that he was not a politician, but a businessman (a very successful one significantly more than his failures). He is definitely no diplomat, which he openly admitted, but given his opponent's track record neither is she.

This by no means endorse the Republican candidate by any stretch of the imagination. The accomplishments of his business successes should be heavily considered by the voters in the United States. The last real true businessman in office was Richard Nixon and if he was honest about the scandal that really marks his presidency; he probably would have been noted in history as one of our greatest presidents.

Reflecting on the election, if the Republicans had a better candidate, he or she would be in the election. I have seen the commercials for the 2016 election and it seems that the Democrat candidate is relying more on personal attacks and past failures she made claiming that they were really successes. As mentioned above, this question really haunts me and should really haunt everyone else considering voting for the Democratic candidate; once again name me three things that she accomplished politically on her own? It is really time to put all the personal attacks aside and stick to the real issues. Please do not count riding her husband's coat tails into the Senate or being former first lady. One last thing to ponder if she was so great at being Secretary of State, why didn't the president fight harder to keep her? Makes one wonder?

As it turned out the United States Presidential election was won by Donald Trump and the Republican Party. Although, this publication primarily covers the 20th Century, the aftermath from the 20th century could be felt in the first part of the 21st century. Whether these results are positive or negative can only be determined over time. Judging his performance over the so-called first 100 days is not a good measuring stick of his performance considering the mess he inherited from the past administration spanning eight years earlier. If one could judge the quality people that he is trying to surround himself; one cannot deny that he is trying to make a real effort to do the right thing for the United States.

The Bible

Chapter 17

God and Religion

The subject of religion and One True God are subjects that seem to be missing in our world despite all the so-called advancements. Normally, the subject is taboo unless a person is going to church or a worshiping dwelling. It seems that we have extremists on both ends of the spectrum when it comes to the question or issue of religion. As we truly examine this issue there seems to be equally an effort in the United States to take God out of everything just as across the world there are religious fanatics looking either push their beliefs on others or kill innocent men, women and children because of a different belief called Christianity. It seems that in a country called the United States, which was founded on Freedom of Religion, Speech and the right to bear arms(weapons), there is an effort to take God out of our National Anthem (Under God) and off that special paper or bank notes worth different denominations called money (In God We Trust). Still worse, to eliminate the privilege and right from our children to pray to their Supreme Being in our schools should be labeled as criminal and against our own Constitution. Having the privilege of attending a Catholic grammar school, we always started the day with prayers and the national anthem. That tradition continued when I attended a public school in junior and senior high schools, with a minute or two to have the same freedom privately.

Still it even gets worse as the analysis goes on to the fools on the hill. They are so busy pushing their constitution and forgetting that they took an oath to defend the United States Constitution, insomuch they should listen to the majority in this country that love and cherish our freedoms. The questions must be asked, does this insult everyone, who fought and died for these rights? What about their families? How about us, who are alive and benefited from their ultimate sacrifice? More importantly, What about God? Who could remember politicians ending their speeches asking God to Bless Them and America? Instead of irresponsibly letting radicals in this country and giving them benefits, why not give the very same benefits to our citizens and children struggling to get an education? Here is a radical idea, LETS BRING GOD BACK IN OUR WORLD and let's start here in the United States. All the evidence and all the truths are in and we need HIM!! Anyone who is opposed to this notion can go back where they came from and push their ideologies on those people.

Since the belief in one God, Entity, Supreme Being/Spirit or what belief system we as human beings subscribe in; there has always been violent acts done in the Deity's name. This would be far from what this Higher Being wants and intended for us as part of His creation. The fact and part that science has played is and has been debatable and for every question answered, there are more questions posed in the present and even more on the horizon. In recent years, it was discovered that there is a DNA trait common to every human being on the planet. If one traces far enough back into history human origins are linked through this DNA.

If one honestly researched history, it has been documented that the Holy Bible is technically the first history book ever written. The fact that civilizations that existed when the book was written supports the events that were reported in the Holy Bible. These civilizations include Greece, Egypt, Rome, countries in Africa and the finding of the Dead Sea Scrolls. The separation of church and state was and is the main goal of almost every so-called government or country in what we refer to and call sarcastically the modern world, which some experts theorized or claim started in the 18th century to the present time. Except for dictatorships and terrorists backed governments in isolated countries, the use of five or six laws given theoretically to Moses several centuries were used as a base of government and laws that are used to this very day.

Looking at the United States objectively since its birth in 1776 has not changed a great deal mainly due to the influences from the 20th century. There is no reason or changes, which to a great deal mainly due to the influences from the 20th century in the concept of separation of state and religion. There is no intention to down play the War of 1812 or the several reasons behind the United States Civil War in the 1860's. These reasons centered around for a host of scenarios, but the main reasons were Freedom of Religion, Heavy Taxation, Economics and The Right to Bear Arms. The Freedom of Speech could be added to the list above, along with the publicized reason of equal rights for all Americans regardless of race or creed.

To continue with the United States, it would be remiss not to document what is and had taken place in the part of the 21st century. First is that fateful and cowardly acts in September 2001 that put North America on the list of terrorist targets. Only someone that is totally ignorant would think that these terrorists' acts were planned at a spur of the moment. Something that elaborate had to take years to plan and put into action. Plus, the fact that terrorism was taken place for decades in the 20th century to isolated parts throughout the world. Religious fanatics from groups to the extent to even some countries would support and give refuge or protection to these same fanatical groups that would have various agendas. These actions have been going on for centuries and it actually started in isolated countries and parts of the world, but because of various reasons these cowardly acts of violence and murdering innocent men, women and children grew to both an epidemic and global proportions. Sadly, virtually no one was safe from the barbaric, uncivilized and senseless acts of violence and were or are exempted from these occurrences.

The issue that seems senseless is that almost every religious faith had humble beginnings; preaching, teaching and promoting love and peace. Then eventually there were an evolution to the complete opposite to people or groups that call or worship God, first by a different name then in a different way. As civilized we think we are because of advancements, this is one consistent constant since the beginning of the One True God Concept. Each seem to have its own period or era, which had violent acts that were contrary to the intentions of the religious concepts originally taught and advocated.

The inescapable fact was the existence of Jesus from Nazareth and his three-year ministry that forever changed humanity and history. The civilizations, which were in existence in that time and era confirms this fact. These civilizations include documentation from the Jewish, Greek, Egyptian and Roman, who had been the most dominating civilization of that era and in control of what is now called the Holy Land. There were other civilizations that also confirms this fact, but they were smaller or in their infancy in comparison to the ones listed above. The fact that there are nearly 1.2 billion Catholics in the world plus other Christian religions and sects that have originated from Jesus' relatively short three-year ministry that can only be best described as a phenomenon and will be hard to emulate again in human history unless it is done by a phenomenon beyond our world.

Although this chapter is supposed to be about God and Religion, its seems more politically oriented than what the original thought was supposed to convey. The old adage 'that there are no atheists in foxholes' only conveys half the thought. With only the real small minority trying to remove God from our lives, how can this be right? Just observe the major retailers' actions in August and September in our immediate past; already setting designated areas for that Holiday called Christmas or more disgustingly called Xmas. Sadly, it is the commercial part of a very great occurrence in human history, but the real crime is that for years the Friday after Thanksgiving, called Black Friday, does not seem to exist anymore. We have seemed to forget that there was a very important birth that took place and as stated earlier there are more than 2 billion people that celebrate that event on a global scale. If one truly examines the New Testament of the Holy Bible, to paraphrase Jesus. He said give Caesar what is Caesar's and God what is God's. One cannot help that we as a society have concentrated too much on Caesar and not enough on God!

Our world and times cry out one thing, God, Please Forgive Us and Come Back! It is time for the majority to stand up and make our feelings known both here in the United States and throughout the world. It is time to kick out the pompous and arrogant fools, who think they are something special and think our world does not need God!

Although there were no direct quotes in this publication except where it was noted, there was research done to confirm the accuracy of the information conveyed. The author would like to acknowledge and thank the following sources. Inclusive to the references include college classes, books and educational articles.

Information Sources
http://www. Usdebtclock.org

http://www.history.com/topics/inventions/invention-of-the-pc

http://energy.gov/articles/war-currents-ac-vs-dc-power

http://www.thefreedictionary.com/information+age

http://www.u-s-history.com/pages/h3974.html

The Holy Bible, Gospel of Saint John

http://overcomeeverything.com/2924/edison-tesla-war-currents/

http://history-world.org/sumeria.htm

http://www.ancient.eu/Mesopotamia/

http://history-world.org/maya.htm

http://www.lost-civilizations.net/mayan-history.html

http://www.greatachievements.org/?id=3659

http://www.greatachievements.org/?id=3661

http://www.aes.org/aeshc/docs/recording.technology.history/radio-television0.html

http://www.biography.com/people/albert-einstein-9285408#!

"Wealth Daily"<wd-e letter@angelnexus, com>

Davis, Ward, President Audio Visual Imagineering

Hubschman, Sanford, Retired

Picture References

001 --- https://pixabay.com/en/
sphinx-egypt-hieroglyphs-temple-1175825/

002 --- https://pixabay.com/en/
egypt-desert-animals-camels-sand-2569182/

003 --- https://pixabay.com/en/
cancun-pyramid-maya-temple-mayan-2269936/

004 --- https://publicdomainvectors.org/en/free-clipart/Mayan-
calendar/53156.html

005 --- https://pixabay.com/en/the-colosseum-roman-italy-2182384/

006 --- https://pixabay.com/en/
washington-monument-sky-clouds-85534/

007 --- https://pixabay.com/en/
aircraft-drawing-design-early-1326276/

008 --- https://pixabay.com/en/
radio-old-tube-radio-nostalgia-1682531/

009 --- https://pixabay.com/en/tv-vintage-old-1005310/

010 --- https://pixabay.com/en/
hand-remote-control-control-select-642138/

011 --- https://pixabay.com/en/cable-distribution-electrical-1868352/

012 --- https://pixabay.com/en/lion-image-7-55-inch-2210947/

013 --- https://pixabay.com/en/satellite-dishes-reception-195132/

014 --- https://pixabay.com/en/
computer-desktop-workstation-office-158675/

015 --- https://pixabay.com/en/satellite-moon-earth-planet-1820064/

016 --- https://pixabay.com/en/easter-easter-candle-cross-2226169/

017 --- https://pixabay.com/en/
madonna-maria-mother-of-god-figure-1396273/

Printed in the United States
By Bookmasters